Knowledge, Productivity, and Innovation in Nigeria

Knowledge, Productivity, and Innovation in Nigeria

Creating a New Economy

Ismail Radwan
Giulia Pellegrini

THE WORLD BANK
Washington, D.C.

ISBN: 978-0-8213-8196-0
eISBN: 978-0-8213-8197-7
DOI: 10.1596/978-0-8213-8196-0

Cover photo: Used by permission from the Women's Technology Empowerment Centre – W.TEC, Lagos, Nigeria

Library of Congress Cataloging-in-Publication Data

Radwan, Ismail.
Knowledge, productivity, and innovation in Nigeria : creating a new economy / [by Ismail Radwan and Giulia Pellegrini].
    p. cm.
Includes bibliographical references.
ISBN 978-0-8213-8196-0 — ISBN 978-0-8213-8197-7 (e-version)
1. Information technology—Economic aspects—Nigeria. 2. Human capital—Nigeria. 3. Education—Economic aspects—Nigeria. 4. Manpower policy—Nigeria. 5. Nigeria—Economic policy. I. Pellegrini, Giulia. II. World Bank. III. Title.
HC1055.Z9I5563 2009
338.9669'06—dc22

2009042590

Contents

Figures

Tables

Foreword

Nigeria has a bold vision of becoming one of the top 20 economies in the world by 2020, as outlined in its "Nigeria Vision 2020" strategy. Although currently eighth in the world in terms of population, the country ranks 41st in terms of GDP and 161st in terms of GDP per capita. Despite being one of the poorest countries in the world, Nigeria is a powerhouse on the African continent by virtue of its size. Its vast oil wealth also promises much in the way of potential finance for development.

How can this enormous potential be realized, and what policies are needed to achieve this ambitious dream of economic growth and prosperity? The authors of this report believe that the goal of becoming a top-20 economy can only be achieved if Nigeria also makes the transition to a new economy based on knowledge, productivity, and innovation that will enable it to be competitive in a 21st century context.

Knowledge has always been central to development. Traditionally, cultures that knew more than others were better able to adapt to their environments, survive, and thrive. In ancient times, knowledge was spread through the most serendipitous ways—from migratory movements to religious pilgrimages, from wars to intertribal marriages—and, thus, traveled across continents. Nowadays, the Internet has become the primary vehicle of knowledge dissemination—almost the entire gamut of human history and knowledge is available in an instant and at little cost through the World Wide Web.

Knowledge is becoming truly global, accessible, and democratic. The impacts of this paradigm shift are all around us. Countries such as the Republic of Korea, India, and the United States of America that can harness the power of new technologies nurture a cadre of knowledge workers that can push the productivity and innovation frontiers. Others that fail to do so remain mired in poverty.

The global financial crisis has shown that countries can no longer rely on narrow and static paradigms of growth, such as Nigeria and its natural resource endowments. The era when natural resources dominated trade has given way to an era in which knowledge resources are paramount. Our world is changing rapidly and those who will be able to acquire, adapt, and utilize new ideas and innovations, regardless of who has invented them, will create tremendous wealth in the process. To achieve Vision 2020, Nigeria needs to move beyond the stop-start development patterns of an oil-based economy to create a stable and prosperous base for a 21st century society built on a critical mass of knowledge workers.

Not since the beginning of the Industrial Revolution has there been a more urgent time to rethink outdated development paradigms. How can Nigeria prepare for this century? What areas must its leaders focus on to achieve the vision of a new Nigeria? This report seeks to answer these questions.

Acknowledgments

This report was written by Ismail Radwan[1] and Giulia Pellegrini.[2] Chukwuemeka Ugochukwu of the World Bank and Anush Wijesinha of Leeds University in the United Kingdom provided excellent research support. Chapter 3 draws heavily on original work completed by Mavis Ampah of the Global ICT group of the World Bank. Ndubuisi Ekekwe, a doctoral student at Johns Hopkins University in the United States, provided valuable input for the preface and insightful comments on an early draft of the report.

The report was written under the guidance of Marilou Uy (Director, Africa Finance and Private Sector Development Department) and Iradj Alikhani (Sector Manager). The peer reviewers for this paper were Itzhak Goldberg, William Maloney, and Vincent Palmade.

The authors received valuable comments and support from the following individuals from the World Bank: Onno Ruhl, Mavis Ampah, Peter Materu, Olatunde Adekola, and Anuja Utz.

---

1. Senior Private Sector Development Specialist, Finance and Private Sector Development, Africa Region, the World Bank, e-mail: iradwan@worldbank.org
2. Junior Professional Associate, Finance and Private Sector Development, Africa Region, the World Bank, e-mail: gpellegrini@worldbank.org

The authors would like to acknowledge the generous financial support received from the governments of Norway, Sweden, and the United Kingdom through the Multi-Donor Trust Fund that has made this publication possible.

Abbreviations

3G	third generation
AfDB	African Development Bank
AIST	African Institute of Science and Technology
BDS	business development services
BPO	business process outsourcing
CBN	Central Bank of Nigeria
CDMA	Code Division Multiple Access
ECOWAS	Economic Community of West African States
EDB	Export Development Board
EU	European Union
FDI	foreign direct investment
GDP	gross domestic product
GERD	gross expenditure on research and development
GSM	Global System for Mobile Communication
GRI	government research institutes
HIV/AIDS	human immunodeficiency virus/acquired immune deficiency syndrome
ICT	information and communication technology
IIM	Indian Institute of Management
IIT	Indian Institute of Technology

IPOS	Intellectual Property Office of Singapore
IPR	intellectual property rights
IT	information technology
KE	knowledge economy
KEI	knowledge economy index
KAM	Knowledge Assessment Methodology
MAN	Manufacturers Association of Nigeria
MDGs	Millennium Development Goals
NACCIMA	Nigerian Association of Chambers of Commerce, Industry, Mines, and Agriculture
NCC	Nigerian Communications Commission
NIPC	Nigerian Investment Promotion Commission
NUC	National Universities Commission
PC	personal computer
OECD	Organisation for Economic Co-operation and Development
PPP	public-private partnership
R&D	research and development
SMEs	small and medium enterprises
SMEDAN	Small and Medium Enterprise Development Agency of Nigeria
SOEs	state-owned enterprises
S&T	science and technology
UBE	universal basic education
USPTO	U.S. Patent and Trademark Office
WBI	World Bank Institute
WTO	World Trade Organization

Overview

Knowledge for Development

Harnessing knowledge for development is not a new concept. Knowledge has always been central to development and can mean the difference between poverty and wealth. The knowledge economy is not just about establishing high-tech industries and creating an innovative and entrepreneurial culture. Economic literature indicates that simply adopting existing technologies widely available in developed countries can dramatically boost productivity and economic growth. This paper highlights the knowledge economy (KE) issues that confront Nigeria and offers policy prescriptions that will allow the country to take advantage of the opportunities available in moving toward a knowledge-based economy.

The Knowledge Assessment Methodology (KAM)[1] developed by the World Bank considers four pillars:

1. Skills and Education
2. Business Environment
3. Information and Communications Infrastructure
4. Innovation System

Using these four criteria, it is clear that Nigeria's progress when benchmarked against other countries remains limited. Oil provides 95 percent of government revenues, while the economy remains predominantly agrarian. The debilitating lack of power has resulted in a shrinking industrial base. Once-widespread industries such as textiles and shoe making have for the most part disappeared. While focusing their efforts on reviving such ill-fated industries, policy makers have often inadvertently overlooked the tremendous potential the country holds in the knowledge economy and its corollary, the service sector. Services are growing rapidly in Nigeria and will form the base for the push toward Vision 2020—becoming a top-20 economy by 2020. In each of the four KAM pillars, there is tremendous scope for creating centers of excellence that can then drive the country's broader transformation.

Skills and Education

Nigeria's ability to create a demand-driven education system that focuses on lifelong learning will determine the country's capacity to embrace the benefits of the knowledge economy. Achieving universal primary education in Nigeria is itself a challenge. Although this is a fight well worth fighting, international experience has shown that even countries without basic literacy for a large part of their population can create centers of excellence in education, as in the case of India. To become a knowledge economy, Nigeria will need to improve the quality and relevance of education, particularly of vocational training, and expand access to tertiary education.

A better education system will allow Nigerian youth to take advantage of economic opportunities and become active players in their own economy. At present, only 16 percent of young Nigerians have a job outside of the subsistence agricultural economy. This situation represents a tremendous waste of young talent and a potential source of conflict. Despite increasing amounts being pumped into education, outcomes have not improved, and the Federal Ministry of Education has described the situation as "not only an educational crisis but a crisis for the nation."

The three key problems of the Nigerian education system are access, quality, and funding. To take advantage of the opportunities offered by the knowledge economy, government can reform the education system by introducing a transparent admissions system, as well as merit-based graduation. Now students pay their way through university and pay for good grades. Gender bias remains a key challenge for Nigeria. This is especially true for young girls in the northern regions. This is not simply a cultural reticence, but tuition, and the costs of books and uniforms, represent a heavy burden for many families. Other countries, most notably Bangladesh, have shown that this situation can be quickly turned around with cash vouchers to encourage families to send their girls to school.

The quality and relevance of education can be improved by ensuring that all teachers are qualified for their jobs and by retraining those who are not. Science, technology, and mathematics all need a boost. The government has started in this area by establishing the Abuja campus of the first African Institute of Science and Technology (AIST). The National Universities Commission (NUC) accreditation system is also strengthening its enforcement of accreditation standards and has sanctioned institutions that could not meet the standards.

There is scope for increasing funding at all educational levels and introducing modern tools and techniques such as computers and the Internet throughout the education system. Internet access in Nigeria's schools remains at half the level of comparator countries like Ghana and the Arab Republic of Egypt. Developing strong synergies between the public and private sectors could deliver better educational services in the realms of training and curriculum development. Following the Korean example, Nigeria could publicly fund basic education and then open up higher levels of education to increased private-sector funding. Industry-led skills development programs could also be replicated throughout the education system. The recently established Digital Bridge Institute aims to do that by providing information and communication technology (ICT) education and training through linkages with the private sector.

The challenges faced by the Nigerian education system are great, but so too are the potential and the scope for meaningful government participation as an architect, provider, and partner, rather than just as a regulator. To improve access, quality, and funding of education, Nigeria must harness the contribution of the private sector. Government can play a catalytic role in the process of building strong public-private partnerships that could provide funds and know-how to improve curricula and realign research priorities. A stronger and continual exchange among schools, universities, research institutions, government agencies, and private firms can help cater to the needs of industries and produce more employable graduates, thus reducing the serious problem of unemployment among Nigerian youth.

By generating a critical mass of educated people whose skills are continually refined through lifelong learning and the progressive upgrade of the education system, Nigeria can build the foundations of a knowledge-driven economy. Coupling its own characteristics—a young, English-speaking population, great natural resource endowments, a lower prevalence of the HIV/AIDS pandemic compared to the average in Sub-Saharan Africa, increasing regional integration through the Economic Community of West African States (ECOWAS), and the largest market in Africa—with a well-thought-out strategy, Nigeria can gradually create the conditions to take full advantage of the new opportunities arising in the global economy of the future.

Business Environment

A good business environment will create strong incentives for the private sector to be innovative, entrepreneurial, and productive. Nigeria's current business environment remains mixed, with the World Bank ranking it 118th out of 181 countries. Electricity is the main bottleneck. Power outages result in losses of almost 10 percent of total sales, despite the fact that almost all (86 percent) of Nigerian businesses have their own generators.

While it is relatively easy to open and close a business and is easy to hire and fire workers, it remains difficult to obtain licenses and register property—making access to land a key obstacle to establishing a business. Although credit to the private sector is growing rapidly, many businesses report that they remain capital constrained. Trading across borders remains cumbersome and problematic.

In order to benefit from the knowledge economy, it is important that businesses can access new technologies. This is especially true for small and medium enterprises (SMEs) that do not have strong linkages to multinationals or international networks. Properly structured in-firm training can overcome such deficiencies, especially if structured around promising clusters.

Over the past few years, Nigeria has made strides in improving the confidence of foreign investors. Creating a one-stop shop to deal with business regulation issues in the form of the Nigerian Investment Promotion Commission (NIPC) has streamlined investments. It is also hoped that a rebranding exercise recently launched by the Ministry of Information and Communication will go a long way toward improving Nigeria's image overseas. This effort could be completed by streamlining the relationship between rules and regulations for investment at the federal and state levels. A regulatory environment that encourages respect for intellectual property rights (IPRs) also helps attract more investors and foreign direct investment (FDI) even outside the telecom and oil and gas sectors, which have received the lion's share of investment in recent years, and need not prevent a certain level of reverse engineering, which Nigeria could benefit from in the same way many successful emerging economies did during their industrial development processes.

Although Nigeria has made some progress in these areas, much more needs to be done. Other countries have improved their business environments at a quicker pace. Nigeria has slipped in international rankings that measure the ease of doing business and remains behind "peers" when assessing its readiness to embrace the knowledge economy through the KAM, mainly because of the country's poor business environment.

Information and Communications Infrastructure

In today's knowledge-based world, ICT plays a central role in boosting productivity and economic growth. An increase of 10 mobile phone users per 100 people has been shown to increase GDP growth by almost 1 percent. And a 1 percent increase in the number of Internet users can boost GDP growth by 4.3 percent.[2]

The best way to encourage a high-quality and low-cost ICT network to develop is by establishing a liberal regulatory structure that allows for competition and private-sector participation. Thanks to accelerated liberalization over the past 10 years, the Nigerian telecom sector has experienced outstanding growth rates in excess of 37 percent. Most of the growth is concentrated in the mobile phone sector (which now boasts 35 percent penetration) and more could be done to encourage land lines, while Internet penetration is only 5 percent.

Although Nigeria has made great strides in this area since liberalizing the sector in the late 1990s, the high prices, still-low penetration rates by international standards, and limited competition in certain areas reflect an unfinished reform agenda that the government should tackle immediately. Increasing the available bandwidth and bringing down tariffs will spur international investment in the sector and help the country's nascent business process outsourcing (BPO) industry. It will also encourage providers to go to rural areas (perhaps with new technologies such as Code Division Multiple Access, or CDMA) that have so far been neglected.

Only when the bandwidth is increased and the price reduced will the stage be set for all other areas of technology uptake, including e-government services, computer ownership, and Internet usage, as well as e-commerce and business solutions. The federal government can promote this evolution by increasing ICT spending, promoting e-government services, and subsidizing information technology (IT) training within the government, as well as promoting ICT literacy throughout Nigeria's schools.

Innovation System

The first step toward adopting an innovation culture is to adopt existing technologies and adapt them to the local situation. As demand exceeds the supply of skilled human resources, and labor rates in Asian economies edge upward, Nigeria has the potential to absorb existing technologies and production systems, especially in the services industries. Nigeria's production systems are far from efficient and there are great potential gains to be achieved simply by moving toward more modern and efficient production techniques, especially in the service sector. In practice, many of these improvements will come through increased FDI in nontraditional sectors, especially ICT, tourism, and financial services.

Nigeria's innovation system is not as well-developed as those of other African comparator countries. The country needs to strengthen the collaboration between its universities and the private sector. Higher education institutions have few formal linkages to industry, and as a result tend to continue teaching outdated materials and producing graduates who are ill-equipped for the working environment. In the 21st century era of the knowledge economy, the state of the art in many disciplines changes at a much faster pace than it did even a decade or two ago. This is especially true in ICT. It is reported that many of Nigeria's universities are still teaching computer languages that are completely obsolete, like Fortran and COBOL.

Nigeria needs to tackle these issues from both sides: challenging universities to adopt and teach new technologies and providing incentives for firm-level technology absorption. The World Bank-financed Science and Technology Education Post-Basic (STEPB) Project (box 2.3) is a useful vehicle for achieving these goals. However, if it is to be successful, it must be supported by increased funding to Nigeria's research institutions. Government could also play a useful role in harnessing the expertise and finances of Nigeria's impressive Diaspora and active business associations.

Charting a Way Forward

This is an opportune time for Nigeria to begin its transition toward a knowledge economy. Furthermore, this paper argues that focusing on key knowledge economy inputs—education, innovation, ICT, and the business environment—can effectively support the country's new growth strategy, Vision 2020. The vision places economic growth at the heart of Nigeria's development. It is backed by the president's seven-point agenda, which looks to increase power production, invest in education and health, and boost agriculture production within the context of a peaceful and corruption-free Nigeria.

The current global financial crisis and the concomitant fall in oil prices registered until recently have shown that this vision cannot be achieved simply by relying on oil extraction. Nigeria's non-oil growth had been on a positive trend until the global crisis hit. In the future, this trend will have to be sustained through an intelligent economic diversification strategy. Given the short- to medium-term limitations in power and transport, the most promising area is the service sector, and more specifically the absorption of ICT. Growing this sector implies embracing the knowledge economy paradigm, developing education and skills, and putting in place a modern communications infrastructure. Freeing up Nigeria's dynamic businesses to create more ICT jobs will also create more opportunities for Nigeria's youth.

Dialogue and partnerships should be used to encourage the development of research communities in order to build the national innovation system. This will help Nigeria attract more FDI and research and development (R&D) resources to establish national centers of excellence. Innovation through adoption and adaptation will boost productivity and growth, and also improve living standards substantially.

The country also needs to invest more heavily in its people. This process has already started, but now the government must focus on ensuring that increased inputs in the educational and vocational training systems are matched by improved outcomes. A major conclusion of this paper is that, while the fight for universal basic education is still ongoing, Nigeria need not wait before attempting to establish centers of excellence. India exemplifies how world-class facilities, such as the Indian Institutes of Management (IIMs) and IT parks can be created and become successful even while a country is still struggling with providing basic literacy for a large part of the population.

To make these goals a reality, Nigeria needs to improve its business environment to attract FDI outside of the oil and telecom sectors. The country will be unable to reap the full benefits of its investment in expanding education, ICT connectivity, or R&D intensity unless its broader institutional and incentive regimes stimulate the most effective use of resources in these areas, permit their deployment to the most

productive uses, and allow entrepreneurial activity to flourish to contribute to Nigeria's growth and overall development.

Launching a Process: Implementing a "Knowledge for Development" Strategy

To transition to the knowledge economy, Nigeria needs to develop a
vision and a sound strategy by setting up a knowledge economy task
force consisting of leaders from various industry sectors, academia, and
government agencies. This exercise will enhance the interaction among
the relevant parties. The task force should identify industries with
potential, highlight key areas for improvement, chart the way forward
through a "knowledge for development" strategy, and foster cooperation
among relevant parties in Nigeria's quest toward a full-fledged knowledge economy. India and its National Knowledge Commission constitute
a source of inspiration.

Learning from Other Countries

The case studies presented in part II of this paper highlight what Nigerian
policy makers can learn from India, China, Korea, and Singapore—four
countries at very different stages in their KE transitions. India, a large
country with an income level similar to that of Nigeria, is widely viewed
as a leader in offshoring, call centers, and software development. Korea
is currently seen as a pioneer in effectively using knowledge for
growth, while Singapore is in the process of developing its pillars in
order to pursue a relatively new strategy in which innovation becomes
the new focus of the economy. China is only in its initial stages of
developing a new strategy for growth through innovation and beginning to invest in knowledge more heavily. It will be beneficial for
Nigeria to observe the methods that have and have not worked for
each country. This analysis can offer many insights into how Nigeria
can develop its own KE strategies.

Although all four countries are at different stages and have followed
different development strategies, some common themes emerge from the
case studies. All four countries have invested heavily in education. Since
the 1950s, India has developed its Indian Institutes of Technology (IITs)
and its IIMs, world-class management and technology training institutes.
In Korea, a strong cultural affinity to education and government deregulation of the sector in the 1980s now allows more than 50 percent of the
population to attend a tertiary-level institute. In Singapore, education is
the government's second-biggest expenditure item. It has preferred a

strategy focusing on all levels of education, leapfrogging other countries (e.g., Sri Lanka) that started out far ahead in terms of literacy rates and development outcomes. Singapore has also decided to augment its national human resources capacity by opening its doors to foreign-born or foreign-trained knowledge workers. This willingness and ability to embrace international expertise, funding, and ideas, is a key component of its success story. In China, 50 percent of university students study a science- or technology-related subject.

All four countries progressively understood the importance of opening their economies. All started by adopting existing technologies rather than moving into innovative or new industries. All have gradually improved their business environments, climbing several places in international indices in recent years. Despite low adult literacy rates in Singapore (roughly at Chinese levels), the country has more than made up for this by attracting international investment and human resources through its excellent business environment, most notably the strong rule of law and regulatory quality.

Information infrastructure in all four countries was promoted through a liberalization of the telecom sectors, starting with Korea in the 1970s. A solid regulatory structure based around market competition allowed the country to achieve the highest broadband penetration in the world. A dedicated public-private partnership fund meant that funding was always available to drive the sector, and government ensured the relevance and commercial orientation of the investment while also securing public-sector backing to achieve social objectives.

Although all four models rely heavily on the private sector, they also involve high degrees of government coordination. Given the four pillars of the knowledge economy—education, ICT infrastructure, the business environment, and the innovation system—the government has a key role to play as an architect of reform. As such, it should focus on creating a level playing field for all stakeholders, while allowing the private sector to participate where competition is possible, e.g., education and ICT infrastructure.

The message for Nigerian policy makers is clear. Government must increase its investment in R&D and public-sector educational institutions, ensuring funding is channeled to high-performing national centers of excellence. This should be done while encouraging linkages between research centers and the private sector to harness private funding of research and education, particularly at the tertiary level.

This process may only be successfully accomplished through a dialogue with all stakeholders and the commitment from government to craft a sound vision and a coherent set of sector plans. It is hoped that this paper will spur this process to allow the country to realize its enormous potential.

Notes

1. Consult the Knowledge for Development (K4D) Web page on the World Bank Web site for a detailed description of the parameters in the KAM's Innovation Index, at http://info.worldbank.org/etools/kam2/.

2. For further information, see "India: The Impact of Mobile Phones," 2009, Vodafone Group and "The Impact of Telecoms on Economic Growth in Developing Countries," 2005, Leonard Waverman et. al.

PART I

Knowledge, Productivity, and Innovation

CHAPTER 1

Why Is Knowledge So Important for a New Nigerian Economy?

What Is a Knowledge Economy?

A knowledge economy is one that creates, disseminates, and uses knowledge to enhance its growth and development. Knowledge has always been at the core of any country's development process. More recently, however, the increased speed in the creation and dissemination of knowledge makes it an even more important ingredient in rapid economic development. Economic growth and global competitiveness are increasingly driven by knowledge (Salmi 2009).

A successful knowledge economy is characterized by close links between academic science and industrial technology, greater importance placed on innovation for economic growth and competitiveness, increased significance of education and lifelong learning, and greater investment in intangibles such as R&D, software, and education (World Bank 2005a). Investing in the knowledge economy means investing in strategies that will bring about significant changes in the way a country can grow because the application of knowledge brings about more efficient ways of producing and delivering goods and services at lower costs to a greater number of people (Salmi 2009).

The first step in becoming a full-fledged knowledge economy is to use and apply global knowledge to local processes to improve development outcomes. The implementation of international best practices will help to spur Nigeria's productivity and competitiveness. Nigeria's firms can reap huge benefits simply by adopting well-known managerial techniques and practices. Governments can consider moving to the innovation stage much later. The importance of knowledge for an economy should not be seen as limited to high-tech industries and cutting-edge research. Instead, how well economies use appropriate knowledge to improve their productivity and increase their welfare is key. Education and skill levels become important sources of growth and competitiveness in the global economy. Coupled with the use of existing knowledge in a variety of circumstances, not just in leading-edge scientific discoveries, they become essential in both "doing things better" and "doing better things" (World Bank 2005a). Nigeria must differentiate among knowledge that is new to the world, new to an industry, and new to a firm. Applying existing knowledge that is new to a firm or new to an industry in the country will reap huge benefits.

Knowledge can mean the difference between poverty and wealth. In order to remain competitive in the global economy of the 21st century, it will be increasingly important to invest in high-quality education and knowledge production, making each sector of a country's economy more efficient. Figure 1.1 illustrates the significant returns that such an investment can create. Countries such as Korea, Ireland, the United States, and the United Kingdom, which have invested substantially in knowledge factors over the past few decades, have experienced rapid and sustained growth and are currently some of the most dynamic and competitive countries in the world, despite the recent slowdown caused by the global financial crisis.

The dynamic process of knowledge and wealth creation raises tremendous possibilities for enhancing productivity and competitiveness. But there is also a risk that countries or firms and organizations that are not able to keep pace with rapid change will fall behind. A country like Nigeria, which is poised to realize faster economic growth and is planning to move to middle-income status, needs to formulate a robust national strategy aimed at enhancing the application and assimilation of global knowledge, industry productivity, and international competitiveness, with the goal of achieving faster growth and reducing poverty (figure 1.2). This should be the beginning of a longer journey that will make Nigeria a full-fledged knowledge economy in the future.

Having eliminated its debt, Nigeria is embarking on a new development strategy that seeks to bring about rapid and sustained growth. The government has outlined its new economic strategy in the president's

Figure 1.1   Strong Links between Knowledge and Growth

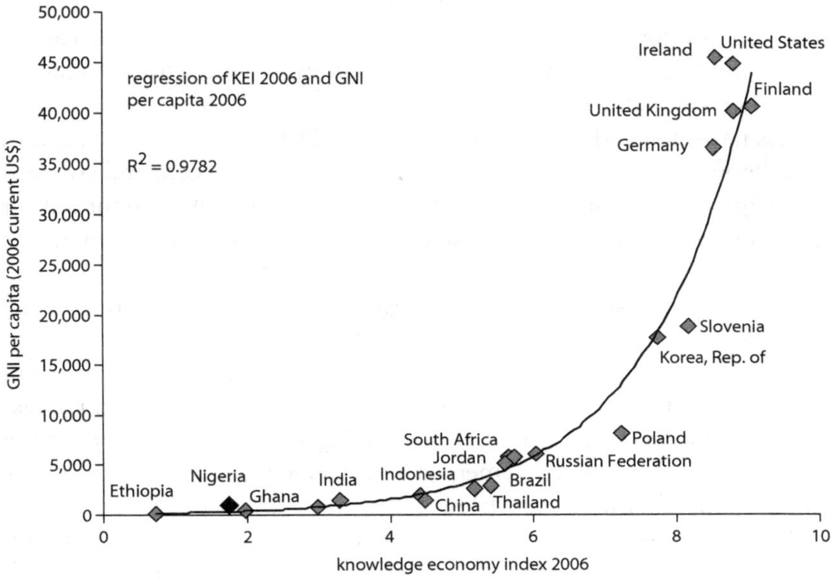

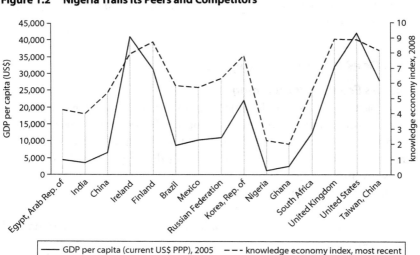

Source: Updated from Dahlman 2003.

Figure 1.2   Nigeria Trails its Peers and Competitors

Source: World Bank Knowledge Assessment Methodology 2009.

seven-point agenda adopted in 2007. The document highlights the need to work on job-creating growth, infrastructure development, and human resource development, among other areas. These are all core areas for improving Nigeria's competiveness through higher industrial productivity and economic diversification.

It is never too early for a country to begin its transition toward becoming a knowledge-based economy. In light of Nigeria's recent and continuing reforms and its ambitions to realize faster growth, it is important for the country's leaders and interested stakeholders to evaluate where the country currently stands on its journey toward a knowledge-based economy and how it can best take advantage of the KE potential. By starting with the assimilation and application of existing global knowledge to improve its productivity and competitiveness, Nigeria need not lose sight of the importance of moving to the knowledge development and innovation stage in the future, and may start doing so in certain sectors of the economy that have already emerged as dynamic performers such as ICT and the film and music industries.

The knowledge economy agenda should first be seen as a productivity-enhancing and competitiveness-promoting agenda. It can then move toward the establishment of a knowledge-creating economy. This paper seeks to benchmark Nigeria's status as a knowledge economy against that of its competitors in Africa and elsewhere. It highlights the specific areas in which the country should improve in order to enhance its international competitiveness, with a view to fully embracing the knowledge economy concept in the future.

What Does This Imply for Nigeria?

Nigeria's Economy Is Changing

In the past eight years, and particularly in the past four, Nigeria has witnessed unprecedented economic and social reforms geared toward setting the country on the path of economic and human development. The government has set out a clear vision charting the way forward—the president's seven-point agenda.

The agenda calls for:

1. Critical infrastructure—particularly improvements in electricity and transport
2. Niger Delta regional development and an improvement in the security situation

3. Food security
4. Human capital development—including increased investments in health, education, and training
5. Land tenure changes and increased home ownership
6. National security
7. Wealth creation

Nigeria is making a bold attempt to reduce its dependence on oil and grow its non-oil economy. The government's first priority is sustainable growth. But growth is not enough. To reduce poverty, such growth will have to involve increased job creation. And job creation is not enough. Nigeria will need to create higher-value-added jobs and ensure that it has the human resources to fill those jobs. In a global and dynamic world, the economies that can remain flexible, adaptive, and innovative will reap the benefits of world trade (box 1.1). This underscores the importance of the competiveness and knowledge economy agenda for Nigeria.

Nigeria's Current Advantages in Embracing the Knowledge Economy

Nigeria's economy is growing rapidly, but remains heavily tied to oil revenues (figure 1.3). High crude oil prices, accompanied by prudent government expenditures, have resulted in significant savings that have been stored in the Excess Crude Account. These funds can be used to diversify the economy and create opportunities for future growth. In terms of education, despite low literacy rates, Nigeria's widespread use of English

---

Box 1.1

Services Take Lead in World Employment

The services sector recorded the highest employment share, equal to 40 percent of world GDP in 2006, with agriculture at 38.7 percent, and industry at 21.3 percent. Services overtook agriculture for the first time in 2006. Roughly 22 million manufacturing jobs disappeared globally between 1995 and 2002, with China losing around 15 million manufacturing jobs. The need to think of innovation in services to keep up with this trend of declining manufacturing and growing services has never been more important than now.

Source: ILO Global Employment Trends 2007.

Figure 1.3   Nigeria Slipping on KE Indicators

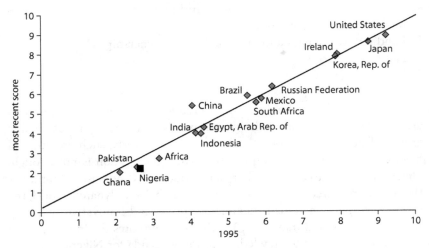

Source: World Bank Knowledge Assessment Methodology 2009.

is an advantage. The country has a free-market economy, a dynamic private sector, macroeconomic stability, and an emerging democratic system. Although the business environment remains challenging, it is gradually improving and remains open to foreign investment and committed to private-sector competition. In addition, the size and balance sheet strength of Nigeria's companies is allowing its private sector to look further afield for opportunities throughout the continent. This business expansion across the continent also spurs demand for liberalized trade and improved infrastructure in Nigeria. These are at the heart of the knowledge economy.

Assessing Nigeria's Opportunities and Challenges as a Knowledge-Oriented Economy

Four Pillars of the Knowledge Economy

The World Bank Institute (WBI) has defined the knowledge economy as consisting of four pillars, which if strengthened can result in growth and development (Nigeria 2009a).

1. **Business Environment:** An economic and institutional regime that provides incentives for the efficient creation, dissemination, and use of existing knowledge

2. **Education and Skills:** An educated and skilled population that can create and use knowledge
3. **Innovation System:** Firms, research centers, universities, consultants, and other organizations that can tap into the growing stock of global knowledge and assimilate and adapt it to local needs and use it to create relevant new knowledge
4. **Information and Communication Infrastructure:** This can facilitate the effective communication, dissemination, and processing of information.

In order to benchmark Nigeria's position in its long-term transition toward becoming a full-fledged knowledge economy, the World Bank's Knowledge Assessment Methodology (KAM) will be used throughout the paper (box 1.2). The KAM includes several quantitative and qualitative variables that compare an economy with its neighbors and competitors in order to determine the areas within the country's economy that are in need of improvement, investment, and

---

Box 1.2

Knowledge Assessment Methodology (KAM)

The Knowledge Assessment Methodology is a tool designed by the World Bank Institute to help countries assess their preparedness to compete in the global knowledge economy. The KAM considers 80 structural and qualitative variables that allow an economy to benchmark itself compared to other countries. This helps countries understand their strengths and weaknesses through a cross-sector approach that considers a variety of factors. The variables are used as proxies for four pillars considered critical to the development of a knowledge-oriented economy: education, economic and institutional environment, ICT infrastructure, and innovation.

The KAM is updated yearly and collects data from World Bank datasets and international literature for 128 countries. Countries are ranked based on the absolute values recorded for each of the 80 variables, and more than one country may receive the same rank (1 = best performer). The scores are normalized (from 0 = worst to 10 = best) for every country on every variable, according to their ranking and in relation to the number of countries in the sample. The score provides an assessment of the performance of a country relative to that of the rest of the sample. For more information on the KAM, see www.worldbank.org/kam

reform. Three variables are chosen as proxies for each of the four pillars that constitute the Knowledge Economy Index (KEI):

- education and skills: adult literacy rate (age 15 and above), secondary enrollment, and tertiary enrollment
- economic and institutional regime: tariff and nontariff barriers, regulatory quality, and the rule of law
- information and communication infrastructure: telephones per 1,000 people, computers per 1,000 people, and Internet users per 10,000 people
- innovation system: researchers in R&D, patent applications granted by the U.S. Patent and Trademark Office (USPTO), and scientific and technical journal articles (all weighted per million people)

Benchmarking Nigeria's Knowledge Economy

Nigeria has been slipping in terms of the knowledge economy since 1995. Figure 1.4 presents country performance in 1995 compared to the present. Countries above the line have improved their performance on the KE indicators. Those below the line have slipped. South Africa and Egypt remain well ahead of Nigeria. Nigeria is ahead of Ghana, although the latter has been improving at a quicker rate. It is interesting to note that some of the world's most dynamic economies, such as China and Brazil, have

Figure 1.4   Nigeria Lags on KE Because of a Weak Business Environment

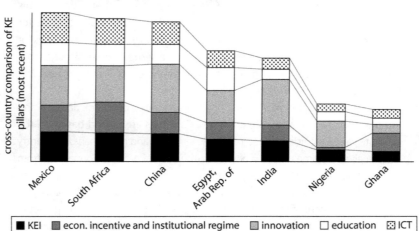

Source: World Bank Knowledge Assessment Methodology 2009.

managed to make the most improvement in their KE indicators (i.e., are farthest above the line).

Nigeria lags behind the more dynamic countries in Africa and Asia because its investment climate remains weak, as figure 1.5 indicates. It is clear that the business environment (the economic and institutional regime) contributes significantly to this poor performance. This situation presents an opportunity as well as a challenge because reforming the business environment usually revolves around "stroke of the pen" types of reforms that can be implemented quickly and easily once government has the awareness and the political will to make them happen. Working on the business environment means addressing tariff and nontariff barriers, improving regulatory quality, and improving the rule of law. These are the areas where Nigeria has slipped significantly since 1995, as highlighted in figure 1.6.

Nigeria's decades of military rule have not allowed policy makers to focus on the KE pillars. However, policy makers now have an opportunity to examine and improve the economic incentive regime as well as tackle other factors, such as the country's education system and physical infrastructure, which have remained stagnant for the past decade (figure 1.6). In the innovation sphere there is welcome news that the sector has largely held its ground, with a consistently high number and quality of journal articles and USPTO patents issued over the years. However, the infrastructure deficit, specifically for ICT and more generally for power and transport, has remained a major hurdle (figure 1.7).

Figure 1.5   Deterioration in the Knowledge Economy Index

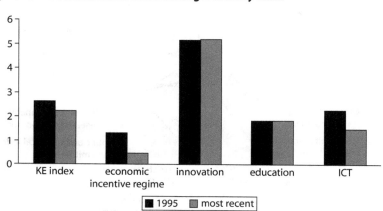

Source: World Bank Knowledge Assessment Methodology 2009.

Figure 1.6   Breakdown of Key KE Indicators for Nigeria (1995–recent)

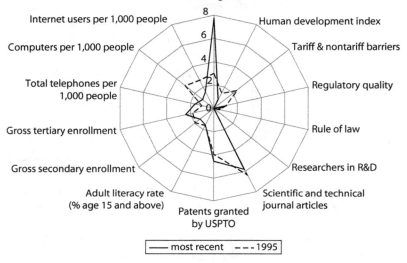

Source: World Bank Knowledge Assessment Methodology 2009.

Figure 1.7   Key KE Indicator Comparisons of Three Countries

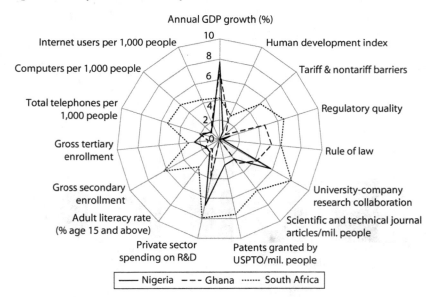

Source: World Bank Knowledge Assessment Methodology 2009.

Nigeria's current economic growth gives policy makers some fiscal space to address KE issues. The one area in which Nigeria has excelled since 1995 is economic growth, despite the recent setback due to the global economic crisis. The debt write-down has seen the country's debt dramatically reduced from close to US$36 billion in 2004 to less than US$3.7 billion in 2007. Continued high oil prices and prudent macroeconomic management have resulted in high growth rates during these years and the accumulation of sizable foreign exchange reserves. This provides some fiscal space to start addressing the backlog of investments required to improve the country's economy (figure 1.8).

Global Rankings

The World Economic Forum's *Global Competitiveness Report 2008* ranks Nigeria 94th out of 134 economies. This places it near to Senegal at 96th place and well behind more dynamic African countries, such as Kenya (93) and Egypt (81). Nigeria's ranking has remained stable, at 93rd in 2007 and 95th in 2006. In the meantime, other countries have rapidly improved their standing.

In the 2007 rankings, Nigeria was placed 48th out of 62 economies in *Foreign Policy* magazine's Globalization Index, while in the 2008 rankings the country was 57th out of 72 countries. The index attempts to gauge how an economy is faring in a globalizing world. The rankings use proxies in areas such as IT, finance, trade, personal communications, politics, and travel. The index indicates that Nigeria does relatively well in terms of trade, FDI, and remittances, but does much worse on technological connectivity and travel. Out of 72 countries surveyed, Nigeria ranks 69th for telephones, 65th for Internet users and secure servers, and 70th for Internet hosts. It also ranks 68th for travel. This is a clear indication of the need to improve ICT infrastructure and usage in Nigeria, a topic taken up in detail in Chapter IV.

Figure 1.7 compares Nigeria's standing on the KE index with other African competitors and finds that it lags behind front-runners like South Africa, but also behind smaller neighbors like Ghana. Supporting the creation of a knowledge economy through innovation, as defined above, will improve the country's competitiveness and put in place a virtuous circle, whereby improved competitiveness in turn will foster more creativity.

Embarking on a Transition to the Knowledge Economy

To make progress on this important agenda, Nigeria will need to define its strengths and weaknesses within the four pillars in order to bring about

Figure 1.8   Nigeria's Economy Heavily Dependent on Oil

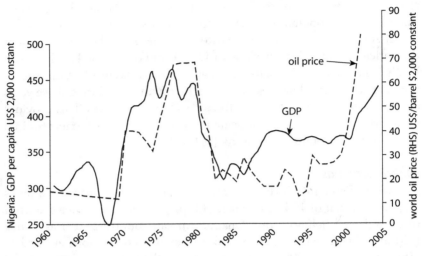

Source: World Development Indicators 2008.

the appropriate reforms to make a successful transition to the knowledge economy. This paper presents a first attempt to highlight these issues within the framework of the four pillars: education, business environment, ICT infrastructure, and innovation.

The following four chapters identify the specific issues and opportunities facing Nigeria in terms of developing quality knowledge economy inputs. Included in each chapter are benchmarking assessments appropriate for each pillar, along with recent developments and policy recommendations. The following chapters include:

- Advancing Nigeria's Education System
- Improving Nigeria's Business Environment
- Expanding Nigeria's Information Infrastructure
- Creating an Innovation Culture

There are many opportunities for Nigeria to make the transition to a knowledge-based economy. The following chapters outline how this could be achieved and aim to give policy makers some food for thought to chart a home-grown path toward Nigeria's new economy.

The second part of the report presents case studies of how other successful countries have managed the transition to the knowledge economy.

These assessments will be useful in helping Nigerian policy makers learn from the various international models that have been successful elsewhere and avoid the mistakes that other countries have made so Nigeria can begin to establish its own strategies in embarking on the knowledge economy revolution.

CHAPTER 2

Advancing Nigeria's Education System

Developing Skilled Human Resources

Highly skilled and flexible human capital is essential to compete effectively in today's world and is a key building block of a knowledge-based economy. Such human capital enables a nation to adopt, adapt, use, and produce knowledge, and becomes central to its development. All levels of education have their roles to play: primary education is the "foundation for lifelong learning" (Utz 2006); secondary education, through general and vocational courses, raises the productivity and trainability of the labor force; and tertiary education, particularly in the sciences, teaches critical thinking and the ability to solve problems and make use of new technologies. This is a necessary, albeit not sufficient, condition for any knowledge economy.

Knowledge has emerged as a critical determinant of competitiveness in today's globalized economy. This is true for developed and developing countries alike, although many of the latter have been lagging in the development of their education systems. Fostering a culture of lifelong learning through formal and informal training is the base from which a country can build an economy capable of competing in the 21st century and meeting the biggest development challenges.

Economic theory also supports the idea of education as a driver of growth and innovation. Lucas' (1988) endogenous growth theory has shown that countries with a larger stock of human capital experience higher growth rates.[1] Investment in education improves human capital and the capacity to innovate. Romer (1990) links human capital to new technology creation and adoption, while Nelson and Phelps (1966) argue that a larger human capital stock aids technological catch-up between lagging nations and more advanced economies. Finally, Artadi and Sala-i-Martin (2003) find that primary school enrollment rates are positively correlated with GDP growth rates in African countries.

Achieving universal primary education is in itself a challenge that many developing countries are grappling with in the context of the Millennium Development Goals (MDGs). Developing countries face enormous challenges in developing their educations systems—from providing universal basic education and tackling gender bias, to increasing access to and quality of education, all the way to strengthening tertiary education to produce a critical mass capable of taking advantage of the technological innovations of this day and age.

Nonetheless, international experience shows that a country need not give up on creating centers of excellence, even as it still struggles to provide a large part of its population with basic primary education. India's experience is very powerful in demonstrating how this can be true. While the country has certainly not given up its fight against illiteracy, it has also understood the importance of creating pockets of excellence, such as the IITs and IIMs, which have become pivot points for the economy as a whole and placed India on the world map for sectors such as computer software and the offshoring service industry.

Many countries, particularly developing ones, must improve the access to, quality and relevance of, and funding for, education in order to produce the flexible labor force that is required to project them into the realm of knowledge economies (Dahlman 2008). Nigeria is one of these countries. As such, it must avoid becoming complacent and read the recent years of steady economic growth as a sign of permanent achievement. What has been accomplished so far could be quickly overturned if strong institutions are not put in place, particularly in the context of the current global financial turmoil and fall in oil prices. Thus, it is paramount that Nigeria focuses on education and invests in the sector. This will help it build the foundations of a strong and diversified economy that could better cope with potential adverse terms of trade and other challenges in the future. In line with President Yar'Adua's seven-point agenda and Vision 2020, better access to and quality of education will help Nigeria improve its non-oil growth prospects, reduce poverty, and increase shared prosperity.

Nigeria's Education System

Improving Basic Education

A better education system will also allow Nigerian youth to take advantage of economic opportunities and become active players in their own economy. At present, only 16 percent of young Nigerians (age 15 to 25 years) have a job[2] (Haywood and Teal 2008). This dire situation is similar to that of many African countries, where overall 72 percent of young people earn less than US$2 a day (World Bank 2008).

Since the return to democracy, the Nigerian government has faced more pressure to improve access to, and quality and funding of education. In particular, the post-basic education segment is rapidly expanding, with a greater number of Nigerians moving into it (World Bank 2006). To the government's credit, progress has been made. Notable achievements, such as the increase in public spending on education as a percentage of GDP (figure 2.1) and the improved access rates obtained through the Universal Basic Education (UBE) program must be acknowledged.

Despite these efforts, Nigeria's education system has not made any significant progress since 1995 when compared to other countries (figure 2.2). Although the country has made some improvements in its education level

Figure 2.1   Rising Public Expenditure in Education with the Return to Democracy[a]

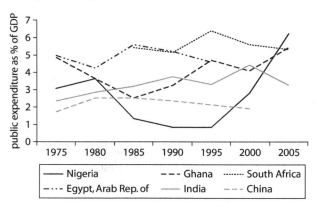

Source: UNESCO, World Bank.
Note: Data for Nigeria for 2000 and 2005 actually record data for 1999 and 2002, respectively, but are used for comparison purposes, due to the paucity of data.

Figure 2.2   Still Further to Go in Education

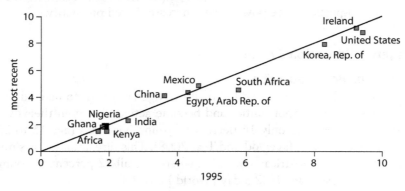

Source: World Bank Knowledge Assessment Methodology 2009.

and quality in absolute terms, these have merely been sufficient to keep pace with other nations. Funding remains low in absolute terms, and is generally input-based (e.g., focused on providing classrooms and textbooks) rather than related to performance and output (e.g., reading and comprehension levels). The 2009 budget provides for 91 percent of capital expenditures to focus on five key sectors, including education, with ₦33.6 billion (approximately US$200 million) (Nigeria, Budget Office of the Federation 2009b). This is a decrease from the ₦47.7 billion (US$300 million) allocated in 2008 (Nigeria, Budget Office of the Federation 2009a). Moreover, just as capital budget implementation remains very low across the board in Nigeria, the education sector seems to be no exception, with a 17.7 percent implementation rate at the end of the first quarter of 2009 (Budget Office of the Federation 2009c). There is little incentive for teachers to perform and to partner with the private sector (World Bank 2006). As a result, Nigeria's educational outcomes still lag well behind those of India, South Africa, Egypt, China,[3] and Mexico, although it is ahead of Ghana, Kenya, and the average for Africa as a whole.

The Nigerian education system is similar to that of many Anglophone African countries.[4] It comprises nine years of basic education—six years of primary school, three years of junior secondary school, and three years of senior secondary school. To these, generally four years of tertiary education are to be added. The responsibility of providing education is divided among the federal, state, and local governments, along with a growing number of private providers. While the federal government is mainly responsible for tertiary education,[5] secondary and primary education are the remits of state and local governments, respectively. Federal education institutions are comprised of 27 universities, 22 colleges of education, and 19 polytechnics (World Bank 2007).[6] There are also 32 state and 34 private universities (Okoje 2008) (see box 2.1).

Improving Oversight of Education

A considerable impediment to the development of the sector has been the lack of reliable data and poor policy coordination. At present, "available educational management data are insufficient to provide the necessary information on which to build effective policies and strategies" (World Bank 2006). Existing mechanisms to collect and analyze

---

Box 2.1

Brief History of Nigeria's Universities

The history of tertiary education institutions in Nigeria is particularly poignant. The first university to be established in Nigeria, following the recommendation of the Elliot Commission in 1943, was the University College of Ibadan. The university opened in 1948 and issued joint degrees with the University of London throughout the 1960s, when other "first-generation universities" focused on educating Nigeria's elites, were also created. "Second-generation universities," which were set up to provide educational opportunities to all, were founded in the 1970s (e.g., Uniben, Bayero University Kano, Unical, Unijos, etc.) and were followed by state universities in the 1980s.

During the years of dictatorship, particularly the harsh decade of the 1990s, many of the best academic minds left the country, funding for education was cut, and the tertiary education system virtually collapsed. The University of Ibadan was stripped of the ability to issue joint degrees with the University of London, while other top universities (University of Nigeria at Nsukka, Ahmadu Bello University, etc.) saw a tremendous decline in standards. The practice of the elite of studying abroad intensified, as did the brain drain, with many students never returning to work at home. With the emergence of democracy in 1999, there has been a surge in the establishment of private universities, although the quality of some is rather questionable. Given that the total number of students has almost doubled (from 744,000 in 1999 to 1.3 million in 2007), the challenges faced by the tertiary education system have been compounded.

Source: Mailafia 2008.

such data should be enhanced and streamlined across the different agencies involved (ministries, quasi-governmental organizations, tertiary institutions, etc.). A better coordinated policy approach would also help harmonize priorities and strategies across the system. For example, science and technology issues and education issues are often addressed in a compartmentalized manner, thus creating either policy gaps or duplication of efforts (World Bank 2006).

In 2007, the Federal Ministry of Education, in its 10-year strategic plan, described Nigeria's education system as a whole as "not only an educational crisis but a crisis for the nation." Nigeria seems to fare substantially worse in most education indicators than African peers like Ghana, Egypt, and South Africa (figure 2.3). Particularly telling are the indicators for adult literacy rates, as well as secondary and tertiary enrollment ratios. Moreover, the figure cannot reflect wide regional and gender differences in the country—completion and enrollment levels are much worse in northern states and among girls. A cross-country comparison of selected indicators (below) highlights some of the pressing challenges that Nigeria must tackle in order to build a knowledge economy and catch up with peers.

Figure 2.3   Nigeria's Education System Lags African Peers

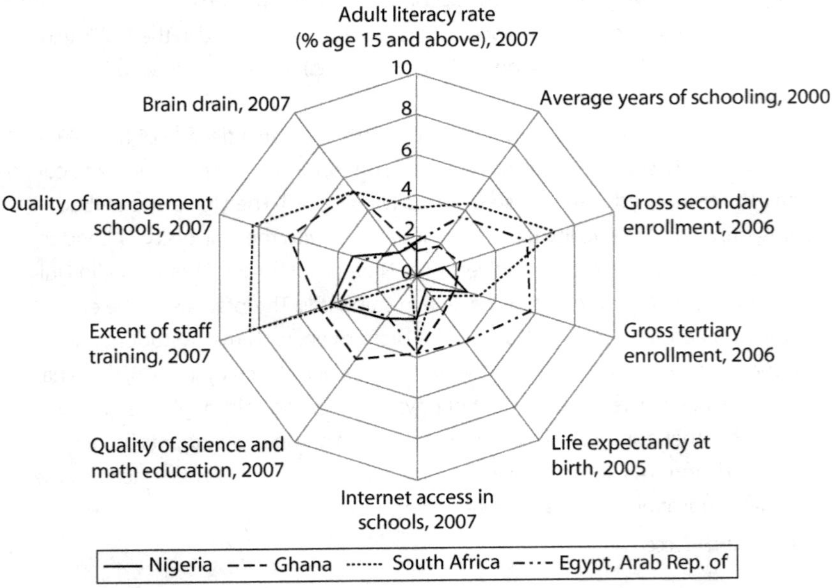

Despite the large increase in tertiary enrollment rates since 1999, Nigeria is still behind in the process of building a critical mass of highly educated people. As figure 2.4 shows, Nigeria is ahead of Ghana, but remains behind competing emerging markets in terms of tertiary enrollment levels. Although this lower enrollment level in Nigeria helps in the short run by avoiding the effective collapse of the university system, which barely copes with its current number of students, this will put the country at a tremendous disadvantage in the future unless improvements are made. Students sit in overcrowded lecture rooms that lack electricity. They are taught with obsolete methods and old books and graduate later than expected due to the strikes and administrative hiccups that affect the system. Reports of corrupt teachers, who demand bribes to pass students or do not show up in classrooms, unfortunately are not infrequent (Walker 2008). The tenure and student admission systems in universities are not entirely transparent or merit-based (Odia and Omofonmwan 2007). Finally, the endemic lack of resources (of universities as well as of students to pay their fees) puts a further cap on numbers. Nigeria should follow the example of other emerging markets. The Ninth Malaysia Plan aims to shape the transformation of the country into a knowledge-based economy by placing particular emphasis on the contribution of the university sector (Salmi 2009).

Science and Mathematics Are Key
Developing a small number of centers of excellence would attract talent and funding. Salmi (2009) argues that developing countries should first focus on "… developing the best national universities possible, modeled

Figure 2.4   Low Tertiary Enrollment Stifles Development

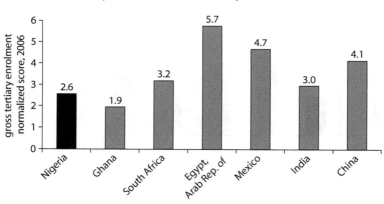

Source: World Bank Knowledge Assessment Methodology 2009.

perhaps [after] the land-grant institutions in the United States during the 19th century or the polytechnic universities of Germany and Canada." By promoting the creation of a few pockets of excellence in the local context, developing countries could put emphasis on the specific learning and training needs of the domestic population and economy. Nigeria could start by nurturing a number of local centers of excellence. Through well-crafted public-private partnerships, these centers would attract talent and funding, especially from domestic or multinational firms operating locally, without causing serious resource diversions away from other key areas of the education system. This would lay the foundation for a stronger tertiary education sector and pave the way for "broader world-class aspirations" (Salmi 2009) later on.

ICT and other modern learning tools are not widespread in Nigerian schools, reflecting the poor infrastructure levels of the country. Figure 2.5 shows how Nigeria lags, by a considerable margin, behind all other comparator countries in terms of Internet access enjoyed by its schools. When considering China and India, the difference is threefold. In such conditions, students do not benefit from the knowledge-sharing properties that the World Wide Web can offer their peers in other countries. A primary tool for knowledge sharing, dissemination, and adoption is missing, and basic IT skills necessary in today's job market are not acquired. This also prevents Nigeria from more aggressively pursuing important opportunities such as the global offshoring business. Undeniably, given the poor state of infrastructure and lack of funding, it is hard for Nigeria to follow the example of countries such as Singapore with its Masterplan for ICT in

Figure 2.5   Tools of Modern Education System Missing

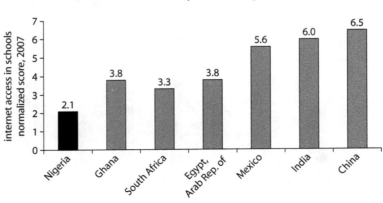

Source: World Bank Knowledge Assessment Methodology 2009.

Education—a plan aimed at incorporating ICT in all school curricula. A first step in this direction could be for Nigeria to put together a strategy for the use of ICT in the education sector. Recent initiatives such as the Nigerian Universities Network project, which aims at connecting several federal and private universities and developing shared infrastructural facilities for cooperation and cost-reduction, represent a good start (World Bank 2006).

Nigeria needs to strengthen the quality of teaching in math and science if it is to become a full-fledged knowledge economy. A sizable cohort of people educated in math and the sciences helps a country internalize technology and innovations developed abroad, and one day make the jump and develop new ones locally. It should be noted, however, that although it lags behind its regional competitor, Ghana, as well as India and China, Nigeria is not at the bottom of the ladder and comes before Egypt, Mexico, and South Africa (figure 2.6). Further proof of this are some notable achievements. At the 17th Pan-African Math Olympiad in 2007, Nigeria's Uchendu Ndubisi clinched the gold medal in the individual competition, while Nigeria as a team came in second, behind South Africa (Mailafia 2008).

Although a strong scientific knowledge base is essential to become a knowledge economy, organizational and other soft skills are also necessary to manage the process. Nonetheless, the quality of most of Nigeria's management schools leaves much to be desired. This is a serious problem that can hamper efforts to move toward a knowledge-based economy, as illustrated by the case of China. China is similarly suffering from poor-quality management schools (figure 2.7). It has been improving fast

Figure 2.6   Science and Math Teaching Must Be Prioritized

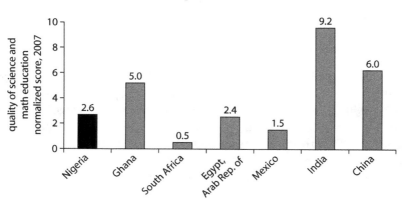

Source: World Bank Knowledge Assessment Methodology 2009.

Figure 2.7   Soft Skills Needed for Knowledge Economy

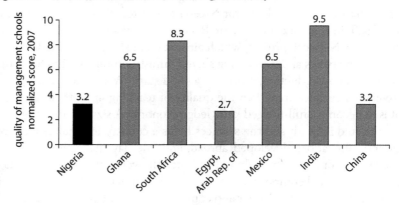

Source: World Bank Knowledge Assessment Methodology 2009.

in the number of highly trained scientists and technicians over the recent years. However, it has not paid sufficient attention to other skills, such as marketing, management, human resource development, foreign language fluency, etc., which are also essential to the development of a more productive knowledge economy. Many observers note that this has resulted in a dearth of Chinese brands. In contrast, India has developed world-class management schools and has the brands and new products to show for it. Nigeria must avoid following the Chinese path of neglecting such skills. Although they may seem less relevant, they are crucial for the smooth management and evolution of a knowledge-driven economic strategy.

Improving Access, Quality, and Funding

The three key problems of the Nigerian education system are access, quality, and funding. Access to education is essential to build a stock of highly skilled people who can turn Nigeria into a knowledge economy. Quality is equally essential. Poor-quality educational programs do not equip people with the necessary skills to compete effectively in today's globalized economy, where advanced technical knowledge is the bread and butter of many industries. Lack of funding deters improvements in standards and impairs the capacity of the education system to be a catalyst for innovation in the country.

Improving Access to Education

Access to education in Nigeria is limited. As previously noted, Nigeria does not fare well on education access indicators when compared to its peers. Moreover, lack of access to education varies widely among different regions and has a strong gender bias. The group facing the lowest level of access is young girls in the northern region, where cultural practices, poor employment prospects, and the cost of schooling have left many at home doing housework or getting married very early.[7] Although enrollment has been improving since 1999, with the concerted efforts of the Universal Basic Education (UBE) program and the funds channeled through the Virtual Poverty Fund following the Paris Club debt relief, much still needs to be done to reach the MDG goal of universal basic education by 2015.

Generally, low enrollment rates and gender bias remain problems for the country as a whole, and not just at the primary school level. At other levels of the education system, gender bias remains strong, with boys greatly outnumbering girls in science and technology colleges (by 81 percent), polytechnics (by 60 percent), and universities (by 73 percent). Low enrollment rates, regardless of gender, also persist throughout the school system, with only 35 percent of those of age being enrolled in junior secondary school (World Bank 2007) and only 14.7 percent of those who complete it moving on to senior secondary education (Billetoft et al. 2008). In addition, enrollment in technical colleges accounts for only 2.6 percent of senior secondary enrollment (Billetoft et al. 2008). Aside from cultural issues and employment prospects, tuition fees, and book and uniform costs, represent a heavy burden for many families, from primary all the way to tertiary education.

Corruption within the education system substantially lowers access. If the practice of paying bribes to teachers (who try to supplement their meager salaries) to pass exams is also counted (Odia and Omofonmwan 2007), the cost of education increases substantially, thus lowering access. This has tremendous implications for building up the highly educated workforce needed for Nigeria to become a knowledge-driven economy.

Providing good-quality, well-targeted, and timely education and skills should be another focus area. School and university programs are often obsolete and make use of outdated books, equipment, and practices, which encourage rote learning and theoretical notions rather than hands-on learning and problem-solving techniques (Odia and Omofonmwan 2007). Underresourced and overloaded curricula and lack of coordination between national education policies and activities that actually receive funding are common in many disciplines, including science and ICT.

In 2006, the Office of the Senior Special Assistant to the President on MDGs alerted the government that more than 40 percent of Nigerian teachers did not possess the National Certificate of Education. The Office of the Senior Special Assistant to the President on MDGs put to use the resources in the Virtual Poverty Fund to retrain 145,000 teachers and recruit 40,000 newly qualified ones (Ibrahim 2006; MDG Monitor 2008).

Improving the Quality of Education

There is a big mismatch between what is taught and the competencies needed in the workplace. This results in many school leavers and graduates being ill-prepared to compete in the job market and causes a shortage of skills in some industries (World Bank 2006). This is partly because strategies for skills development tend to be "reactionary," rather than "proactive," and do not target expected areas of growth. This is the case in the banking sector, for example, where industry-specific skills are lacking and demand is very high. As a result, the Lagos-based industry has been recruiting aggressively from the City of London among Nigerians in the Diaspora. The industry is prepared to pay generous salaries to attract home those who have become quite skilled in their years working and studying abroad. Thus it is very important that labor market trends are systematically studied in order to provide policy makers with the necessary information to make informed choices on funding and curriculum development. As highlighted earlier, the data currently available is just not sufficient to guide policy makers.

Nigeria's scientific and technological training has received a boost in recent years. In 2000, the Federal Ministry of Education launched a "Master Plan for Technical and Vocational Education Development, 2001-2010," in an attempt to tailor technical education to the demand of the labor market and provide more hands-on training. Under President Obasanjo, a National Council for Science & Technology was established to spearhead the effort. The Abuja campus of the first Africa Institute of Science and Technology (AIST) was also initiated. The AIST initiative is an example of a public-private partnership, with the objective of establishing institutes of science and technology all over Africa, inspired by the Massachusetts Institute of Technology in the United States and the IITs in India.[8] In 2006, the government identified 43 goals for a new science and technology framework. This is a welcome step forward, but more effort needs to be put into reprioritizing these goals more effectively.

There is a need to resolve the lack of coordination and dialogue among existing research institutions, universities, government ministries, and agencies. This would serve to target interventions to areas of growing market demand (Billetoft et al. 2008). Research institutions currently seem to set their work targets by totally disregarding market needs, thus operating in a vacuum, without interaction with industries. A study of the African Development Fund (2005) concluded that technical education in Nigeria "is unable to respond to the changing labor market requirements because of its present supply-driven orientation." Another study, by the Industrial Training Fund and the Nigeria Employers' Consultative Association (2007) finds that staff members do not possess the required competencies (particularly ICT and communication skills) in 26 percent of the interviewed organizations.

Putting in place a stronger national qualification accreditation system would help ensure graduates of any institution possess the skills that their qualifications formally indicate they have. The quality of university degrees is often well below international standards, despite Nigeria's tertiary level accreditation system[9] (box 2.2). The same poor quality of

Box 2.2

Nigeria's Accreditation System

To improve the quality of its universities, Nigeria introduced an accreditation system for academic degrees and programs in 1990. Reliant entirely on local resources and experts, the system is run by the National Universities Commission (NUC) and determines whether a certain degree program meets the conditions set in the Minimum Academic Standards by NUC. In this way, the NUC aims to certify the level of competency that students should attain in their areas of study and inform employers, parents, students, and the international community. The assessment covers the areas of academic programs, staffing, physical facilities, financing, resource materials, and employers' ratings of graduates (if available). Although the use of local experts only makes the system well-tailored to the Nigerian context, the lack of international benchmarking deters from its efficacy in conveying information about standards and making reliable international comparisons. Nonetheless, NUC's efforts to provide feedback on its findings to universities and to advise institutions on how to improve on any deficiencies should be acknowledged. In 2007, 26 of the 872 programs (3 percent) offered by universities were denied accreditation status following NUC's assessment and had to cease admitting students.

Source: www.nuc.edu.ng

teaching, equipment, and programs is found in technical education, for which the National Board for Technical Education is responsible. The establishment of a National Vocational Qualifications Framework, as envisaged in the master plan, could help resolve these problems.

Nigeria could take inspiration from international experience in monitoring the quality of teaching and learning. For example, Singapore's Quality Assurance Framework for Universities (see country case studies) has been successful in tracking quality enhancement. Nigeria could also strengthen regional initiatives to monitor educational quality, such as the West African Examinations Commission; expand the coverage and scope of work along the lines of the Southern and Eastern African Consortium for Monitoring Educational Quality; or could participate in international assessments, such as the Trends in International Mathematics and Science Study, the OECD's Programme for International Student Assessment, or the International Adult Literacy Survey (Utz 2006).

Developing strong synergies between the public and private sectors could deliver better educational services. Given the mismatch among the quality of education, the relevance of research work, and the needs of the economy, better coordination through intense dialogue and collaboration with the private sector is key to producing a workforce that possesses relevant skills for the local economy and is flexible enough to take advantage of the changing opportunities of today's global economy. Industry-led skills development initiatives through some private-sector "champions" could pave the way to apply this approach more broadly to the whole education system. The private sector could help by providing information on current technology trends and skill requirements; by offering job placement opportunities for students; and by participating in public-private partnerships for training. On the other hand, stronger synergies would benefit the private sector in terms of availability of better training courses for employees, given the poor quality of some of those offered at present (Iarossi 2008).

Some interesting partnerships between the public and the private sectors are beginning to emerge but need strengthening. The recently established Digital Bridge Institute provides ICT education and training under the initiative of the Nigerian Communications Commission (NCC), through linkages with the private sector. Vocational enterprise institutions and innovative enterprise institutions offer vocational, technical, technological, and professional education and training at the post-basic level (Billetoft et al. 2008), in partnership with the private sector. The Industrial Training Fund provides short-term courses and apprenticeship programs for industry, as well as administers the Student Industrial Work

Experience Scheme. In addition, it operates the Center for Industrial Training Excellence and is about to establish a hospitality and catering training center with the assistance of the government of Singapore (World Bank and AfDB 2008).[10] These institutions represent notable initiatives and it is important that such public-private partnerships are cultivated and developed. The partnership with Singapore is also very valuable. Nigeria could learn much from the country's industrial training system and the Singapore Workforce Development Agency, which has a mandate to enhance workforce skills through market-driven continuing education.

Increasing Funding for Education

Funding for the upgrade of the education system and the increase in enrollment rates is another key challenge for Nigeria. At present, funding from government is not performance-based and does not leverage partnerships with the private sector. Private funding in education concentrates mainly on private universities, where enrollment in science and technology subjects is low (World Bank 2007). Moreover, government funding for university research is too low to attract industry partners into R&D agreements, unlike Singapore, Korea, and other more advanced knowledge economies. By losing out on these highly beneficial partnerships, Nigeria is constraining its potential in breaking into lucrative, job-creating industries. Considering India's IT and other outsourcing industries, strong synergies between the public and private sectors are essential to create a critical mass of people who have trained at dedicated institutions that receive generous funding and are committed to research. In this way, India began its still-continuing evolution away from an agricultural society and into a knowledge-driven economy (Wijesinha 2008).

A boost in funding for education could also come from channeling money from Nigerians in the Diaspora. Nigerians abroad already contribute to funding the education of their loved ones in Nigeria by regularly sending money home. These remittances are used to pay for fees, books, and uniforms. A more concerted effort, including increasing the number of philanthropic programs, as well as attracting Nigerian entrepreneurs abroad to invest in education activities and transfer foreign know-how back to the homeland, could gather considerable amounts of funding as well as technical inputs.

Nigeria can learn from the achievements and mistakes of other countries in boosting funding for education, striking a balance between public and private sources. For example, the Korean government focused mainly on providing primary education as a public good, increasing public financing of education 27-fold over 40 years. Subsequently, it moved funding "downstream," toward higher education, but also worked toward building into the whole system strong curricula and R&D-oriented activities to ensure industry needs were catered to and private funding was enticed. The latter progressively overtook government funding as the largest source of financing for R&D activities. Singapore and its venture capital funds could also be of inspiration as a means of attracting R&D funding, although this would admittedly be more difficult given Nigeria's current business climate.

Partnerships with the private sector and a performance-based incentive system could help improve the funding and quality of education. Currently, the Nigerian education system does not adequately reward excellence. Funding is not performance-based. Different government agencies (e.g., Federal Ministry of Education, National Board for Technical Education) are responsible for allocating predetermined amounts of government funds to different educational institutions. This does not encourage a drive toward results in terms of teaching excellence and research output. On the contrary, it discourages the most motivated students or researchers, who every year leave Nigerian educational institutions for foreign ones. By tapping into the experience of other countries, as well as the lessons learned from in-country projects, such as the World Bank Science and Technology Education Post-Basic (STEPB) Project (box 2.3),

Box 2.3

STEPB Project

The Science and Technology Education Post-Basic (STEPB) project of the World Bank aims to provide "merit-based catalytic funding" to produce more and better qualified science and technology graduates and higher-quality research, particularly for the IT and IT-enabled services sector. The project has three main components, which attempt to:

1) provide peer-reviewed and competitively awarded grants to improve the quality of federal post-basic education science and technology institutions;
2) support the emergence of a number of centers of excellence among promising STEPB institutions; and
3) strengthen strategic planning, management, and monitoring and evaluation in STEPB education in Nigeria.

(continued)

Box 2.3 *(Continued)*

The project aims at prompting real change in the way education is provided in science and technology subjects and in the way it is funded. The project brings into the picture the missing actor in the Nigerian education system—the private sector. By fostering linkages between industry and academia, and creating competition among institutions through the provision of competitively awarded grants, it hopes to encourage innovation in teaching and learning practices, as well as in research output.

Source: World Bank 2007.

some pilot schemes could be devised to introduce performance-based incentive systems in education.

Nigeria can also learn from India's challenges to ensure that the move toward privately funded education does not increase inequality. The increase in privately funded institutions and programs in India has resulted in lower access for the poor (Kingdon 2007) and in a "lopsided" system, characterized by great regional imbalances (D'Costa 2003). Given the already large differentials in funding, and therefore access to and quality of education, in different Nigerian states, it is paramount that the government addresses this from the very start to avoid exacerbating inequalities and encouraging excessive migration to the few, better-served areas that are already under population pressure, especially Lagos.

More attractive returns to education could also prompt more people to enter the education system. A recent study of the Nigerian labor market (box 2.4) finds that returns to education have fallen between 1999 and 2006[11] (Haywood and Teal 2008). The returns are lowest for those employed in agricultural activities, slightly higher for the non-agriculture self-employed, and highest for wage earners.[12] Nonetheless, over the survey period they have been falling for wage employment,[13] as has been the probability of obtaining a wage job for any given level of education. In addition, only 16 percent of youth (aged 15–25) have a job[14] and an estimated 50 percent to 60 percent of graduates from tertiary institutions cannot find an adequate job upon completion of their studies (World Bank 2006), so it is not surprising that people lack incentives to acquire additional education. This has a tremendous impact on Nigeria's current and future development prospects and could effectively prevent the country from building the critical mass of human resources needed

Box 2.4

Nigerian Labor Market

Data from the 2003/2004 Nigeria Living Standards Survey and General Household Survey of the Nigerian National Bureau of Statistics show that the Nigerian
labor market is characterized by 60 percent who are self-employed, 25 percent
who are out of the labor force, 10 percent who are employed for wages, and
5 percent who are unemployed. The proportion of the active population (15–65
years) with a wage job has fallen from 14.2 percent in 1999 to 8.8 percent in 2006.
Half of all formal wage employment remains in the public sector.

At the same time, there has been a shift into family agricultural activities—the
only sector that registered a rise in employment. Nigeria has thus shown the
opposite trend of other African countries, such as Ghana, Tanzania, and Uganda.
Such a shift has also caused a worsening of gender discrimination in the job
market. Given that the gender differential in earnings is lowest in wage employment (25 percent) and more than doubles (57 percent) for women employed
in agriculture, this shift into family farming activities has implied an increase in
average earning differentials by gender.

Source: Haywood and Teal 2008.

for Nigeria to become a knowledge-driven economy. One of the corol-
laries of better returns to education is an increase in people's willingness
to pay higher fees to attend good schools. This would result in higher private funding for education, generating a virtuous circle of opportunities
for the sector.

Summary: Improving the Nigerian Education System

The challenges faced by the Nigerian education system are great, but so
are the potential and scope for meaningful government participation as
an architect, provider, and partner, rather than just as a regulator. In order
to improve access to, and quality and funding of education, Nigeria must
harness the contribution of the private sector. Government can play a catalytic role in the process of building strong public-private partnerships
that could provide funds and know-how to improve curricula and realign
research priorities. A stronger and continuous exchange among schools,
universities, research institutions, government agencies, and private firms
can help cater to the needs of industries and produce more employable

graduates, thus reducing the serious problem of unemployment among Nigerian youth. By generating a critical mass of educated people whose skills are continuously refined through lifelong learning and the progressive upgrade of the education system, Nigeria can build the foundations of a knowledge-driven economy. Coupling its own characteristics—a young, English-speaking population, great natural resource endowments, a lower prevalence of the HIV/AIDS pandemic than other parts of Sub-Saharan Africa, increasing regional integration through ECOWAS, and the largest market in Africa—with a well-thought-out strategy, Nigeria can gradually create the conditions to take full advantage of the new opportunities arising in the global economy of the future.

Notes

1. While theory supports this, it should be noted that the empirical debate seems to be still open. See Wijesinha 2008.
2. This statistic excludes youth employed in family farming activities.
3. It is interesting to note that China, compared to all other countries in the figure, including the most developed economies at the top, has been progressing most rapidly in the past decade.
4. Egypt, Ghana, and South Africa, used as comparator countries below, all have the same basic education system as that prevailing in Nigeria.
5. The federal government typically shoulders about 20 percent of total educational expenditures, while state and local governments bear 80 percent. The federal government also provides additional funding for the UBE program, the Education Trust Fund for physical infrastructure, and other funds from the Debt Relief Gains.
6. The federal government also runs about 120 federal secondary schools.
7. According to the MDG Monitor (2008), only 65 percent of Nigerian children complete primary schooling. Only 57 percent of girls in the northern region of Nigeria are enrolled in primary school (World Bank 2006), while only one-fourth of those of age make it past secondary school. In contrast, more than half get married before age 15, according to UNICEF.
8. The Abuja campus is to be built adjacent to the Abuja Technology Village, an initiative that aims to attract the best brains in biotechnology, pharmaceutical, and IT research, as well as private investment. Other recent research initiatives are the center of excellence for software engineering created in Jos with World Bank support and the ICT Skills Development Centre, being developed through the Digital Bridge Institute. A number of other research institutions predating these are scattered around the country and operate

mainly with government support. Many donors, including the World Bank, UNESCO, AfDB, etc., are also providing support in science- and technology-related projects. See, for example, the World Bank Science and Technical Education at Post-Basic Level (STEPB) project.

9. Consequently, international firms cannot use this system to benchmark Nigerian graduates nor can international tertiary institutions do so. Indeed, it is more common to find many Nigerian students who start their undergraduate degrees (or even secondary schools) abroad, than to see students moving on to graduate studies at universities in the United Kingdom or United States, after having studied in Nigerian universities. This is by no means rare but it certainly was much more frequent in the 1960-80 period, when Nigerian universities were considered some of the best in Africa and many of the economic and political elite of today benefited from a sound university education at home, before proceeding to graduate degrees abroad.

10. In addition, other partnership programs include the Nigerian Institute of Welding in Delta State—a collaboration between the Nigeria Delta Development Authority and a South African partner; and the Shell Youth Development Scheme—a collaboration with Shell Oil, the Nigerian Opportunities Industrialization Centre, and Imo State Technological Skills Acquisition Centre. The Nigerian Association of Small Industrialists, the Nigerian Association of SMEs, and Julius Berger Construction Company also provide training (Billetoft at el., 2008).

11. The study finds that the registered rise in earnings for all types of jobs from 1999 to 2006 has been only due to the improvement in macroeconomic conditions in Nigeria. On the contrary, Iarossi et al. (2008) find that one more year of schooling increases wages by 3–5 percent, putting Nigeria on par with other African countries. Nonetheless, the sample used in the Investment Climate Assessment is biased toward larger, urban-based firms and, indeed, the study finds that firm size is a more significant determinant of earnings. Studies by Fox and Oviedo (2008) for 20 other African countries (excluding Nigeria) and by Söderbom at al. (2008) for Kenya and Tanzania also side with the 2008 Investment Climate Assessment in determining a positive effect of education on earnings.

12. For wage earners, returns to education are twice as high as for those employed in agriculture activities.

13. The data show that returns to education for wage earners were higher in 1999 than in 2006.

14. This excludes family farming activities.

CHAPTER 3

Improving Nigeria's Business Environment

High Cost of Doing Business in Nigeria

A country's business environment is crucial for innovation and entrepreneurial development. It determines whether there are strong incentives for individuals to identify market opportunities and create wealth, jobs, and economic growth. An enabling environment that makes it easy for individuals to start up businesses, run them, sell them, and fold them if they are not successful, is one that fosters national economic growth. There are numerous indices that can benchmark Nigeria's standing in this area.

The Economist Intelligence Unit's *Global Outlook* report ranks Nigeria at 76 out of 82 countries surveyed and characterizes Nigeria's business environment as "very poor." The World Bank's *Doing Business 2010* ranks Nigeria at 125 out of 181 countries. This puts it ahead of countries like India (133) and Brazil (129), but behind more dynamic countries such as China (89), Zambia (90), Ghana (92), Kenya (95), and Indonesia (122).

Why does Nigeria have such a poor business environment? What are the factors behind such low global rankings? What impact does this have on the knowledge economy? And how can Nigeria turn this situation around? These are some of the questions this chapter will answer.

The costs of doing business in Nigeria are high. An adverse business environment can add substantial production costs to firms and stifle innovation and entrepreneurship. It is estimated that the manufacturing sector in Nigeria has to bear additional indirect costs amounting to 16 percent of sales because of bottlenecks in the business environment. Losses due to power outages amount to 10 percent of sales, while production lost while in transit (4 percent of sales) is also significant (table 3.1). These losses affect different types of firms in different ways. Electricity is more of a problem for small- and medium-size firms that cannot easily afford to install and run generators to produce their own power. On the other hand, products lost while in transit due to spoilage affects large firms to a much greater extent as these firms typically service a much wider area.

In comparison to other countries, firms in Nigeria face higher indirect costs (figure 3.1). This is largely due to electricity-related losses. In contrast, Nigerian firms have similar indirect costs resulting from corruption and crime as compared to other countries.

Major Constraints to Business in Nigeria

Electricity, finance, and transport are perceived as the major constraints to doing business in Nigeria, according to a World Bank Group Enterprise Survey that asked Nigerian managers to name the major constraints to doing business (figure 3.2). The perception of other obstacles varies across firms. While electricity appears to be a challenge for all firms, its impact is more significant in the manufacturing sector. Access to finance and its cost appear to affect small and medium firms more significantly than large firms, as well as firms located in less industrialized states. Domestic firms complain more about access to finance than do international ones.

In the manufacturing sector, more than 50 percent of firms perceive access to and the cost of finance, as well as the lack of electricity, as the three most important constraints to their operations. Transportation, the macroeconomic environment, access to land, tax rates, corruption, and crime appear as second-tier concerns (table 3.2). While electricity, finance, transport, and access to land appear to be serious constraints, corruption, crime and tax rates are not perceived as so severe by Nigerian firms, compared to those in other countries (figure 3.3).

Electricity

Electricity is perceived as the main bottleneck. In Nigeria, power outages result in losses equivalent to 10 percent of total sales. Almost all Nigerian

Table 3.1 Indirect Costs—Manufacturing Sector

Indirect costs as % sales	TOTAL	Exporting zone		Firm size			Ownership		State	
		Yes	*No*	*Small*	*Med.*	*Large*	*Foreign*	*Domestic*	*More industrialized*	*Less industrialized*
Electricity	**9.8**	9.3	9.9	10.2	9.3	5.3	10.3	9.8	9.8	9.7
Bribes	**1.7**	2.8	1.5	1.5	2.2	0.9	0.4	1.7	1.7	1.6
Production lost while in transit	**4.1**	7.3	3.6	3.3	5.2	11.6	1.7	4.2	3.8	4.9
Theft, robbery, or arson	**0.3**	0.3	0.4	0.3	0.4	0.4	0.3	0.3	0.3	0.5
Total indirect costs	**15.9**	19.7	15.3	15.3	17.2	18.3	12.7	16.0	15.6	16.8

Source: Nigeria 2008—Enterprise Surveys.

Figure 3.1   Indirect Costs—Manufacturing Sector, Country Comparisons

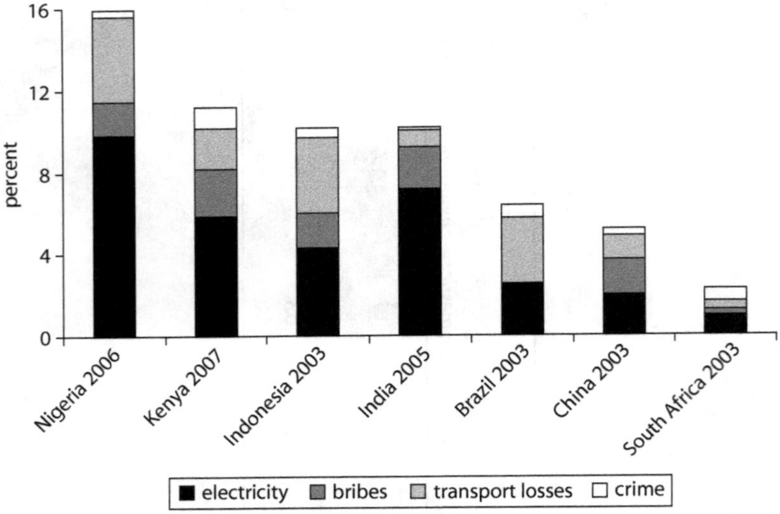

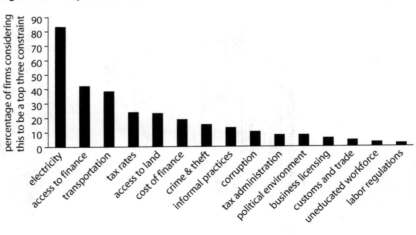

Source: Nigeria 2008—Enterprise Surveys.

Figure 3.2   Major Perceived Constraints

Source: Nigeria 2008—Enterprise Surveys.

firms (96 percent) experience power outages (table 3.3). On average, such outages last 196 hours per month, or about eight days. Large firms and firms in the manufacturing sector appear to be more adversely affected by such outages. Faced with this situation, 86 percent of all firms

Table 3.2 Percentage of Firms Reporting Major or Very Severe Constraints—Manufacturing Sector

Constraint	TOTAL	Exporting zone		Firm size			Ownership		State		State	
		Yes	No	Small	Med.	Large	Foreign	Dom.	More industrialized	Less industrialized	Better regulatory environment	Worse regulatory environment
Electricity	**81**	78	81	82	79	76	100	81	79	84	85	76
Access to finance (e.g., collateral)	**56**	33	60	65	37	14	32	56	53	63	59	52
Cost of finance (e.g., interest rates)	**50**	36	53	58	34	23	66	50	48	57	55	45
Transportation	**33**	24	35	32	35	29	70	33	30	40	28	39
Macroeconomic environment	**30**	28	30	27	37	25	25	30	33	22	29	31
Access to land for expansion / relocation	**29**	19	30	32	21	19	58	28	27	33	32	25
Tax rates	**27**	18	28	27	27	13	32	26	26	29	36	16
Corruption	**24**	8	27	28	17	9	36	24	24	26	33	14
Crime, theft, and disorder	**20**	17	21	22	17	11	25	20	19	24	20	20
Practices of competitors in informal sector	**19**	20	19	21	15	9	34	19	20	18	22	16
Tax administration	**18**	20	17	18	18	2	32	17	17	18	22	13
Business licensing and permits	**14**	14	14	16	12	0	13	14	11	22	17	12

(continued)

Table 3.2 Percentage of Firms Reporting Major or Very Severe Constraints—Manufacturing Sector (Continued)

Constraint	TOTAL	Exporting zone		Firm size			Ownership		State		State	
		Yes	No	Small	Med.	Large	Foreign	Dom.	More industrialized	Less industrialized	Better regulatory environment	Worse regulatory environment
Political environment	13	9	13	13	13	0	25	13	13	12	20	5
Inadequately educated workforce	6	10	5	6	6	2	20	5	5	8	7	4
Telecommunications	5	2	6	6	5	3	20	5	3	11	7	3
Labor regulations	5	9	5	5	6	0	13	5	5	5	9	2
Customs and trade regulations	4	10	3	3	7	1	13	4	5	4	5	3

Source: Nigeria 2008—Enterprise Surveys.

Figure 3.3 Top Constraints in Nigeria—International Comparison

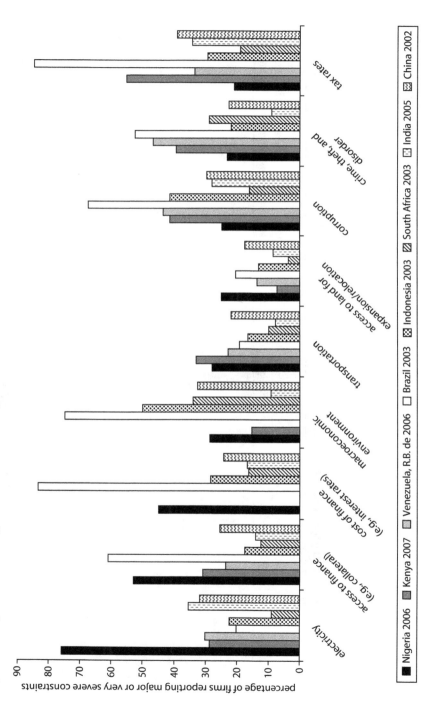

percentage of firms reporting major or very severe constraints

electricity
access to finance (e.g., collateral)
cost of finance (e.g., interest rates)
macroeconomic environment
transportation
access to land for expansion/relocation
corruption
crime, theft, and disorder
tax rates

■ Nigeria 2006 ■ Kenya 2007 ■ Venezuela, R.B. de 2006 □ Brazil 2003 ⊠ Indonesia 2003 ⊠ South Africa 2003 ⊞ India 2005 ▨ China 2002

Source: Nigeria 2008—Enterprise Surveys.

Table 3.3 Frequent Power Outages Hamper Businesses

Indicato	TOTAL	Firm size			Ownership		Industry			State	
		Small	Med.	Large	Foreign	Dom.	Manuf.	Retail	Other	More industrialized	Less industrialized
% firms experienced power outages	**96**	96	95	100	92	96	98	96	93	97	93
Average duration of outages per month (hours)	**196**	198	186	223	125	197	238	188	150	212	169
% firms with own generator	**86**	84	89	97	86	86	86	85	92	87	84
% electricity coming from own generator	**61**	61	61	61	70	61	61	N/A	N/A	63	55

Source: Nigeria 2008—Enterprise Surveys.

have their own generators, which produce, on average, 61 percent of their electricity needs. Although they face the most significant outages, large firms have lower electricity-related indirect costs. This is explained by the fact that 97 percent have their own generators. Power outages vary by state. In Kano, total outage duration averages 393 hours per month, equivalent to 16 days. In Abuja, total outage duration averages 127 hours per month, equivalent to five days.

In comparison to other countries, the percentage of firms experiencing power outages is highest in Nigeria (table. 3.4). As a consequence, generator ownership is higher in Nigeria than in all other comparator countries. Owning and maintaining a generator is an extremely costly affair. It is estimated that self-generated electricity in Nigeria costs between six and 10 times more than that sourced from the grid. This makes all but the most essential and competitive businesses financially unviable, and deters potential entrepreneurs from starting businesses.

Finance

Access to finance, and to a lesser extent the cost of finance, are perceived by Nigerian firms as the second most important constraints to doing business. Capital is a key input to any business. And an efficient financial system that is able to allocate financial resources quickly and cheaply to their most productive uses is an essential part of a growing knowledge economy. For Nigerian firms, both the Enterprise Survey data and other indicators suggest that finance imposes important constraints on business expansion.

Access to and the cost of finance do not impact all firms equally—the smaller the firm, the bigger the problem in terms of access to and the cost of finance (figure 3.4). Domestic firms complain about access to finance

Table 3.4   Nigerian Businesses Face Worst Electricity Constraints—International Comparison

Indicator	Nigeria 2006	Kenya 2007	Venezuela, R.B. de 2006	Brazil 2003	Indonesia 2003	South Africa 2003	India 2005	China 2003
% firms experienced power outages	96	85	21	64	48	N/A	77	N/A
% firms with own generator	86	70	N/A	17	39	10	59	19

Source: Nigeria 2008—Enterprise Surveys.

Figure 3.4   Access and Cost of Finance in Nigeria

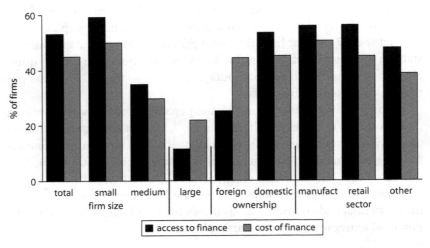

Source: Nigeria 2008—Enterprise Surveys.

twice as much (53 percent) as do foreign firms (25 percent), which often have access to external financing. Similarly, small firms report this as a constraint more often (59 percent) than do medium (35 percent) and large ones (11 percent). Access to finance seems to be more of a problem in less industrialized states (60 percent) compared to more industrialized (49 percent). Across states there is also a significant variation of perceptions in regard to the cost of finance. For example, 77 percent of the firms in Bauchi perceive it as a major constraint, compared to 20 percent in Sokoto.

Business owners in all other comparator countries are markedly less likely to cite finance as an obstacle (figure 3.5). In international benchmarking, only Brazil has a worse perception of access and cost of finance (61 percent and 83 percent, respectively).

The banking sector serves very few businesses in the manufacturing sector (figure 3.6).[1] Nigerian entrepreneurs rely predominantly on internal funds and retained earnings (70 percent) as well as on purchases on credit from suppliers and advances from customers (25 percent). Only a very small proportion of businesses borrow money from their family and friends (4 percent). It is striking that the formal financial sector—banks and other financial institutions—are only utilized by 1 percent of Nigerian businesses. As one would expect, larger firms tend to borrow more from the formal sector. Nonetheless, even the largest firms rely heavily on retained earnings rather than on seeking bank financing. Only 2 percent of

Figure 3.5   Firms' Perceptions of Financial Sector—International Comparison

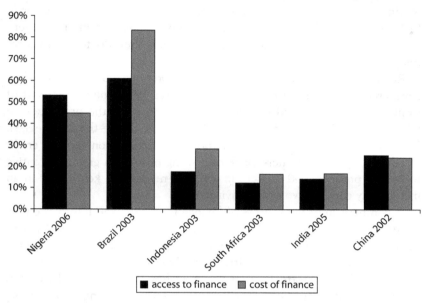

Source: Nigeria 2008—Enterprise Surveys.

Figure 3.6   Nigerian Businesses Largely Funded from Retained Earnings

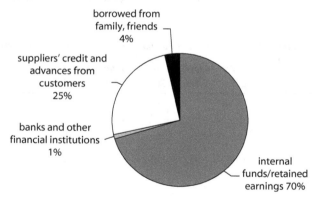

Source: Nigeria 2008—Enterprise Surveys.

medium and large firms borrow from banks, and less than 1 percent of smaller firms do so. This drastically limits the development of innovation and entrepreneurship in Nigeria.

Nigerian businesses rely on retained earnings for long-term financing. When it comes to longer-term financing, entrepreneurs in many countries rely on friends and family acting as business angels and venture capitalists willing to risk their own resources to back promising new ventures. In Nigeria, instead, business owners rely more heavily on internally generated resources for long-term financing than they do for short-term financing.

Reliance on internal sources of finance is pronounced in Nigeria when compared to the rest of the developing world. While only 1 percent of formal-sector firms in Nigeria access bank borrowing, the proportion in China is more than a quarter and in India it is close to one-third (table 3.5). Businesses in those countries also do not rely as heavily on supplier credit or advances from customers. Bank borrowing provides a greater incentive to deliver products and services in a timely manner—a key metric in an increasingly competitive global environment.

A comparison of the sources of finance for formal and informal enterprises shows that entrepreneurs in the informal sector face a similar situation and adopt similar strategies to those in the formal sector. The degree to which informal businesses mirror formal ones in Nigeria is remarkable. Both formal and informal enterprises rely heavily on retained earnings and internal funds for both short- and long-term financing. While informal businesses cannot issue new debt or equity on the capital markets, most formal businesses do not do so either. Nigeria's capital markets lack depth. Informal businesses are also less likely to secure financing from

Table 3.5   Sources of Financing in the Formal Sector—International Comparison

Percentage of short-term financing from	Nigeria 2008	Brazil 2003	China 2003	India 2005	Indonesia 2003	Kenya 2007	S. Africa 2003
Internal funds/ retained earnings	70	44	13	47	38	73	66
Borrowed from banks and other financial institutions	1	30	27	32	16	7	17
Purchases on credit from suppliers and advances from customers	25	15	2	9	4	17	12
Borrowed from family, friends, and other informal sources	4	5	8	9	20	3	1
Issued new equity/debt	–	4	12	2	2	–	1

Source: Nigeria 2008—Enterprise Surveys.

banks than their formal counterparts, although even the latter find it difficult to access credit.

An international comparison underscores the lack of depth of the Nigerian financial sector (measured by M2/GDP). Dynamic economies such as Malaysia and South Africa are at 123 percent and 60 percent, respectively, while Nigeria at 18 percent remains below the sub-Saharan Africa average of 30 percent.

Banking sector. The Nigerian financial sector is dominated by large, local commercial banks (figure 3.7). Through a successful consolidation process, the Central Bank of Nigeria (CBN) requested all deposit banks to raise their minimum capital base from ₦2 billion (US$13 million) to ₦25 billion (US$164 million) by the end of 2005. This process resulted in a reduction in the number of banks in Nigeria from 89 to just 24. In the process of meeting the new capital requirements, banks raised the equivalent of about US$3 billion from domestic capital markets and attracted about US$652 million in FDI into the Nigerian banking sector.

Banking consolidation, with its accompanying race to raise capital, prompted banks to increase their leverage as a result of their dramatically increased capitalization and the need to generate returns to shareholders. On one hand, this produced greater competition, pushing banks to expand into new geographic areas, offer new products, and start providing credit to customers who were previously rationed out. From December 2003 to June 2009, credit to the private sector as a percent of GDP increased by

Figure 3.7   Nigeria's Financial Sector Dominated by Banks

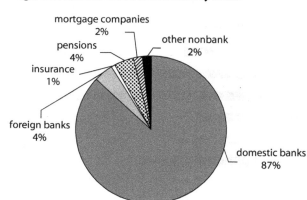

Source: Central Bank 2006.

more than 600 percent, reaching ₦8.6 billion (US$55 million). The period
between June 2006 and June 2008 registered the fastest growth, and saw
the number of loans and advances increase by 297 percent (Lovegrove and
David 2009). On the other hand, this was mostly accounted for by the
growth in loans to the financial sector (mainly for banks' share purchases
or "margin loans"), which grew by an astounding 735 percent, and few
resources followed to the real sector. Moreover, Nigeria remains behind
its regional rival South Africa and other peers among emerging market
economies in credit extended to the private sector as a percentage of
GDP (figure 3.8).

Nigeria's banking sector crisis, which unfolded in August 2009, has
shown the sector to be undercapitalized. Several banks were revealed to
have serious liquidity and insolvency problems. The high capitalization
levels and low levels of nonperforming loans that had been present in
the past were simply a result of bank managing directors (MDs) and
CEOs taking advantage of weak accounting standards and weak supervision (figure 3.9). The practice of margin lending, coupled with poor
corporate governance, insider and related party lending, and overcon-
centration of credit into the oil and gas sector made a number of banks
accumulate bad loans on their books. In five of these institutions, nonperforming loans amounted to ₦943 billion (US$6.2 billion), out of the
total ₦1.14 trillion (US$7.6 billion) estimated to be in the banking sec-
tor (CBN 2009). As a result, the CBN had to inject liquidity into the
five distressed banks in August 2009. The crisis has highlighted the need
to strengthen corporate governance and enhance financial reporting
requirements in the sector.

Figure 3.8   Nigeria's Real Sector Starved for Credit

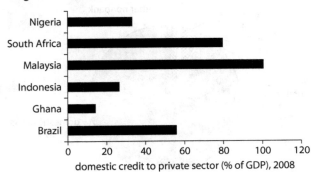

Source: World Bank, International Monetary Fund.

Figure 3.9   Nigerian Banks Well-Capitalized

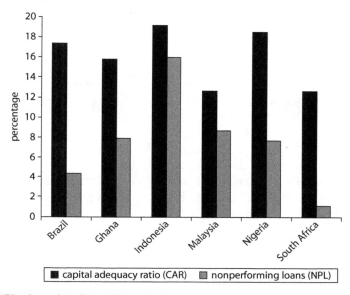

Source: IMF baseline analysis of Financial Sector, October 2007.

The clean-up of the Nigerian banking sector should set the basis for stronger intermediation and wider availability of credit for Nigerian firms going forward. Following the consolidation exercise and bank recapitalizations, Nigeria's banks should emerge with stronger balance sheets going forward. They will also be under more pressure to develop their asset base and search for new and profitable loan markets. By pairing this with stronger and better enforced corporate governance, accounting, and auditing standards, problems associated with the lack of trust that has pervaded the banking business, especially lending operations, should improve. This, in turn, should make more credit available to SMEs.

At present, access to finance by SMEs in Nigeria remains very low. Only 8 percent of Nigerian firms in the manufacturing sector have an overdraft and only half that amount has access to lines of credit (table 3.6). Without such facilities, many firms experience constrained growth and difficulties managing their cash flow, while they are forced to rely more heavily on retained earnings and trade finance. In contrast, more than two-thirds of South African businesses have an overdraft or line of credit, and more than one-third have access to loans. Similar figures are recorded for Brazil and India. Even African peers like Kenya and Ghana are ahead of Nigeria in terms of access to formal credit.

Table 3.6   Access to Credit—International Comparison

% firms with**	Nigeria	Kenya	Ghana	South Africa	India	China	Brazil
Overdrafts	8	21	13	68	53	25	74
Line of credit or loan	4	25	17	38	36	92	35

Source: Nigeria 2008—Enterprise Surveys.
Note: For South Africa, India, China, and Brazil, lines of credit are included in "overdrafts," and not with "loans."
** Weighted average used for Nigeria and Kenya.

What is interesting is that foreign firms located in Nigeria also have better access to overdrafts and lines of credit compared to domestic firms. Foreign firms utilize both facilities about five times more than domestic firms, according to the *Nigeria 2008—Enterprise Surveys.*

Collateral requirements of Nigerian banks remain high and dramatically reduce demand by the private sector for credit. Every loan over ₦10 million (US$64,000) must be collateralized with land or buildings.[2] Loans to informal firms are more often secured against the personal assets of the owner, usually his or her house. As a result, close to 80 percent of loans to Nigerian enterprises require collateral (table 3.7). The value of collateral required ranges from 135 percent to 161 percent of the loan value for formal and informal firms, respectively.

Banks also find it difficult to lend in the absence of a reliable borrower history. This forces banks to require collateral to mitigate against adverse selection and moral hazard problems. At present, the CBN holds information on a limited number of borrowers on its Credit Reporting Management System. The first licenses have recently been granted to a handful of private credit bureaus. This should greatly improve the coverage of existing and future borrowers' histories. Many of these new bureaus are exploring the possibility of introducing biometric identification to make up for the lack of a standard national identification card system (Isern et al. 2009).

The cost and duration of the loans that are available also remain inadequate. Average lending rates in the formal sector were more than 14 percent in 2007, while inflation was 6.6 percent. In 2008, lending rates soared to around 24 percent, and inflation rose into double digits. High and volatile inflation and high real interest rates can deter borrowers from taking out a loan. Moreover, Nigerian entrepreneurs often cannot get loans with maturities that exceed two years. Loans in China and India are available for twice as long, while South African entrepreneurs are able to

Table 3.7   Collateral—Formal Sector versus Informal Firms

		Formal	Informal
Percentage of firms whose loans required collateral		79	83
Value of collateral required (percentage of loan)		135	161
	Land, buildings	66	40
	Machinery and equipment	23	8
Type of collateral required	Accounts receivable and		
(% of firms with affirmative	inventories	24	21
answers)	Personal assets of owner		
	(house, etc.)	37	81
	Other	8	0

Source: Nigeria 2008—Enterprise Surveys.

secure loans of almost six years (Iarossi et al. 2008). This allows South African business owners to plan with more certainty and provides them with the financial capacity to overcome short-term challenges in business performance or the broader macroeconomic climate.

The great majority of Nigerian firms would like increased access to bank financing. More than 70 percent of the businesses interviewed in the *Nigeria 2008—Enterprise Surveys* say they would like a loan. But when asked why they did not apply for one, they cite high interest rates (20 percent) and collateral requirements (20 percent) as the main reasons.

Beneath this aggregate picture, however, the reasons for not applying for a loan differ greatly by firm size. First, almost 80 percent of small firms that do not have access to bank finance would like to have it, while only 20 percent of large firms currently without a loan would like to have one. Second, smaller firms are much more affected by complex loan application procedures (22.9 percent) and unattainable collateral requirements (22.2 percent) than larger firms are (5.8 percent and 3.3 percent, respectively). Close to 55 percent of loan applications from small and micro enterprises are rejected because of unacceptable collateral or co-signer requirements. A higher percentage of smaller firms (20 percent, compared to 14 percent of large firms) also complain that interest rates are not favorable—a reflection of the fact that banks view smaller firms as more risky and often charge them higher interest rates.

In many sectors in Nigeria, competition is artificially restricted by high barriers to entry and the high costs of operating a business. The administrative hassles of doing business in Nigeria are high as are the initial investment costs. Firms that are able to navigate the tricky administrative and infrastructure issues are able to make large profits without the need to expand market share or overextend themselves. However, small firms that would like to expand their businesses are severely credit constrained.

The importance of access to finance for the productive sector of an economy is evident from China's success story. China's dynamic economy has been expanding at double-digit rates largely because of the strength of its private sector. Many formal Chinese firms borrow from banks or issue new debt and equity on the capital markets. China has been able to transition from a command economy to one reliant on family businesses and finally to an economy with a maturing private sector in which less than 8 percent of firms rely on family, friends, and other informal sources of finance. Nigeria has made significant gains in establishing its government debt market, but the development of the corporate debt market is still in its infancy.

As the Nigerian non-oil economy expands,[3] a growing proportion of businesses will need access to bank financing. This signals the need for technical assistance programs in the banking sector to streamline and downscale lending, especially to small- and medium-size businesses. It also points to the need to work with SMEs through business development services providers to support them in putting together business plans and loan applications. Another challenge for Nigeria is how to expand credit to the private sector while controlling risk through improved banking supervision and enhanced corporate governance in the sector.

Transportation and Customs

Transportation emerges as the third most important constraint to business. Transportation problems generate indirect costs on the order of 4 percent of total sales, making it the second most important indirect cost behind electricity. The main cause of such costs is breakage or spoilage of goods (3.2 percent) while in transit. This should not be surprising given the very small share of roads in Nigeria that are paved (estimated at around 15 percent in 2004, compared to 80 percent in China). Yet road transport remains a major means to supply factories. Almost 70 percent of manufacturing firms in Nigeria have their inputs delivered by road.

Efficient customs procedures are important for firms that use a significant proportion of foreign inputs. Nigerian firms import an average of 10 percent of their inputs, with large firms importing 15 percent and foreign firms importing 39 percent. Only 16 percent of firms import directly, and it takes approximately 13 days for imports to clear customs. Exporting is a speedier process, taking on average seven days to clear customs. In comparison to other countries, the number of days needed to clear customs is high. Kenya, Brazil, and India report waiting times to clear customs approximately equivalent to those of Nigeria, while Indonesia, South Africa, and China report much lower waiting times (figure 3.10).

No comparator country requires more documents for both importing and exporting than Nigeria (figure 3.11).

Figure 3.10   Nigerian Traders Face Lengthy Delays at Port

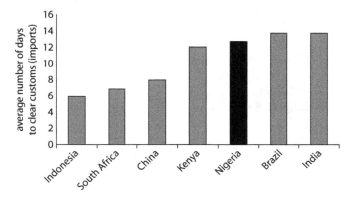

Source: Nigeria 2008—Enterprise Surveys.

Figure 3.11   Trading across Borders—International Comparison

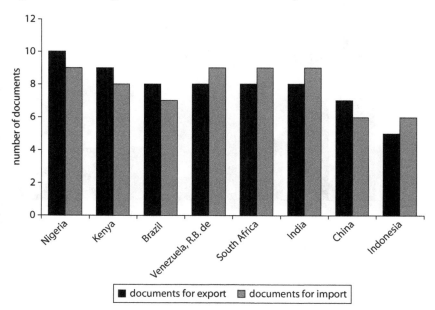

Source: World Bank Doing Business Indicators 2008.

Finally, of all comparator countries, Nigeria remains the most expensive location from which to ship exports or bring in imports. It costs US$1,730 and US$2,450 to ship a 40-foot container for export or import, respectively (figure 3.12).

In summary, transportation emerges as an important constraint because it generates significant indirect costs of doing business. While customs and trade regulations are only perceived by 5 percent of firms to be a major or very severe obstacle, this is in all likelihood connected to the relatively low number of manufacturing firms in Nigeria that trade across borders. For those that do trade, customs appears to be a significant obstacle to business, both in terms of costs and time.

Tax, Land, and Crime

Taxes are relatively low. About one in five Nigerian firms identified tax rates as a significant constraint to business, ranking it the fourth most important constraint. In international comparisons, a higher percentage of firms complain about tax rates in other countries. Using the Doing Business database, the overall tax rate paid by firms in Nigeria is

Figure 3.12   Typical Charge for 40-Foot Export and Import Container

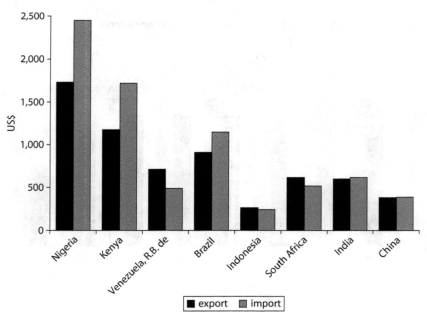

Source: Nigeria 2008—Enterprise Surveys.

the lowest of the comparator countries (figure 3.13). Thus, it would appear that tax rates in Nigeria are not a major bottleneck. The likely reason for it to be ranked as high as it is by enterprises interviewed in the *Nigeria 2008—Enterprise Surveys* is that most of the surveyed sample is composed of small firms, which enjoy fewer exemptions and have a higher effective marginal rate of taxation. Moreover, they are likely to spend a relatively larger proportion of their management and staff time in completing tax-related paperwork.

Land remains a key bottleneck. Access to land was identified by 25 percent of firms as a significant constraint to business, particularly for small firms, as well as for foreign firms. Table 3.8 takes a closer look at the reasons that may justify this perception. The two main reasons why land is perceived as a constraint are the cost of land and the procurement process. According to the survey, 25 percent of firms have tried to acquire new land in the previous three years, and 39 percent of those firms identified access to land as a major or very severe obstacle. Furthermore, even firms that are successful in acquiring land identify it as a major or very severe constraint—almost a third of successful buyers still report access to

Figure 3.13   Composition of Taxes—International Comparison

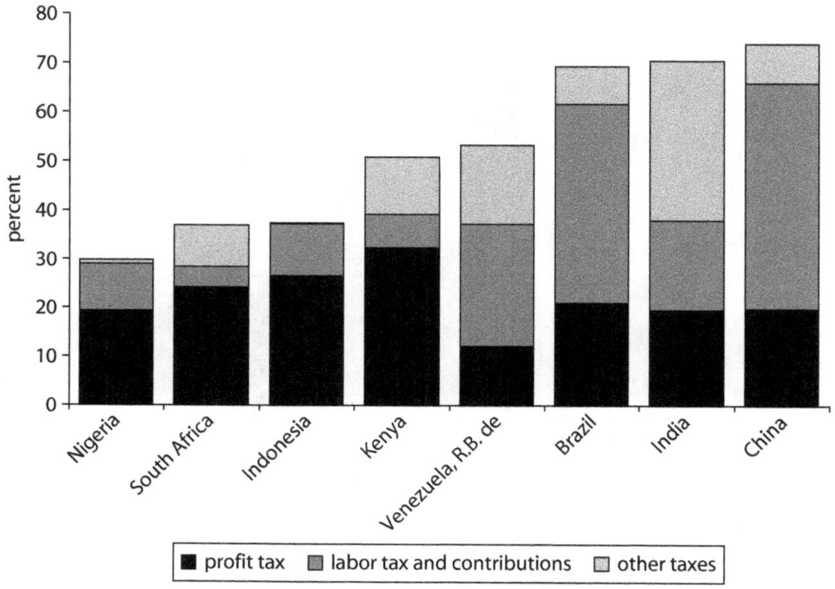

Source: Doing Business 2010.

Table 3.8   Reasons Access to Land Is Perceived as a Major or Very Severe Constraint

Percentage of firms that identify this as reason for access to land for expansion/relocation to be an obstacle	TOTAL	Firm size			Ownership		Industry			State	
		Small	Med.	Large	Foreign	Dom.	Manuf.	Retail	Other	More industrialized	Less industrialized
Cost of land	**92**	92	90	100	89	92	97	85	88	92	91
Procurement process	**70**	71	68	67	89	70	68	72	72	69	72
Availability of infrastructure	**47**	46	51	29	46	47	47	46	46	45	49
Small size of land ownership	**39**	37	47	49	51	39	32	44	48	34	46
Government ownership of land	**39**	37	45	80	18	39	38	37	43	45	31
Disputed ownership	**35**	33	42	69	53	34	28	32	48	32	39

Source: Nigeria 2008—Enterprise Surveys.

Note: Table includes only firms that perceived access to land to be a major or very severe constraint.

land as a major or very severe obstacle. While the cost of land, which is the primary reason why access to land is an obstacle, is an area where intervention is difficult, the procurement process could be significantly improved. It is expected that, as more titled land becomes available, its price will fall as there remains a large premium for formally titled land over informal land.

Corruption and crime. Corruption is perceived to be a serious constraint to business by 25 percent of firms. In an international comparison, a higher percentage of comparator countries' firms report corruption to be a serious constraint. Bribes account for some 2 percent of total sales, which is more or less in line with comparator countries (figure 3.3). Table 3.9 shows that only 44 percent of firms believe that government officials use a consistent and predictable interpretation of the law. This uncertainty may be closely linked to corruption. Small and medium firms perceive corruption to be more of a problem, and a third of all firms report informal payments or gifts to be common to "get things done" regarding customs, taxes, licenses, regulations, etc., while only 25 percent know in advance the amount of payment needed. When a government contract is at stake, firms expect to have to pay some 5 percent of its value in informal gifts or payments in order to secure it.

Firms are often required to pay kickbacks when requesting any licenses. The percentage of firms asked for a bribe when requesting a construction permit or an operating license is 50 percent and 40 percent, respectively (table 3.10). With the exception of construction permits, this problem affects small and medium firms to a greater extent, which may justify their higher perceptions of corruption.

The court system is another institution where corruption is a problem. Table 3.11 shows that firms do not have much confidence in it: only half of firms believe the system to be fair, impartial, and uncorrupted, and only three out of four believe the courts are able to enforce decisions. Clearly, the problem appears to be not so much at the post-decision stage, but at the pre-decision stage, with almost 60 percent of firms considering the process slow and expensive. This conclusion is reinforced by the fact that, while 4 percent of firms had payment disputes in the past two years, just over half were taken to court. This is not surprising. According to the World Bank's *Doing Business 2010*, enforcing a contract through a legal process involves 39 separate procedures, takes 457 days, and costs one-third of the contract amount. Shortening and simplifying this process through a commercial court

Table 3.9 Perception of Government and Regulations—All Formal Sectors

% firms that agree with statement	TOTAL	Firm size			Ownership		Industry			State	
		Small	Med.	Large	Foreign	Dom.	Manuf.	Retail	Other	More industrialized	Less industrialized
Consistent and predictable interpretation of the law	**44**	39	58	74	40	44	43	46	42	46	39
Informal payments/gifts commonplace	**33**	35	29	24	45	33	31	31	38	31	37
Advance knowledge of informal payment/gift	**25**	26	21	19	26	25	26	22	25	25	24
Percentage of annual sales spent on informal payments/gifts	**2.0**	2.0	2.3	0.7	0.7	2.0	1.7	2.0	2.4	1.7	2.4
Percentage of contract value paid to secure contract	**5.3**	5.6	4.7	2.0	4.8	5.3	5.5	4.0	6.0	4.0	7.5

Source: Nigeria 2008—Enterprise Surveys.

Table 3.10 Percentage of Formal Sector Firms Asked for Informal Payments when Making Requests

% firms that have been asked for informal payments when requesting:	TOTAL	Firm size Small	Firm size Med.	Firm size Large	Ownership Foreign	Ownership Dom.	Industry Manuf.	Industry Retail	Industry Other	State More industrialized	State Less industrialized
Telephone connection	**24**	27	20	11	58	24	15	32	29	19	36
Electrical connection	**39**	42	32	10	57	39	35	40	43	38	42
Water connection	**33**	35	30	11	68	32	24	42	37	29	39
Construction permit	**53**	51	56	67	79	52	51	42	59	50	57
Import license	**33**	48	12	35	71	31	24	26	65	23	52
Operating license	**40**	47	28	10	53	40	36	42	45	37	46

Source: Nigeria 2008—Enterprise Surveys.

Table 3.11 Perception of Court System—All Formal Sectors

Characteristics of the court system	TOTAL	Firm size			Ownership		Industry			State	
		Small	Med.	Large	Foreign	Dom.	Manuf.	Retail	Other	More industrialized	Less industrialized
Fair, impartial, and uncorrupted	**53**	52	57	61	48	54	53	46	59	53	55
Quick	**41**	41	41	54	46	41	38	39	47	42	40
Affordable	**41**	38	49	67	58	41	38	40	45	43	38
Able to enforce decisions	**75**	75	77	84	75	75	75	79	74	75	76
Percentage of firms with payment disputes in the past 2 years settled by third parties	**4**	3	6	6	8	4	3	5	4	4	4

Source: Nigeria 2008—Enterprise Surveys.

system or alternative dispute resolution mechanism should be a priority for the government.

While corruption may be perceived as a major bottleneck in Nigeria, there are several countries that are viewed as more corrupt and the country has made improvements in this area in recent years. Transparency International's Corruption Perceptions Index (CPI) attempts to quantify the degree of corruption as seen by business people and country analysts. It ranges between 10 (highly clean) and 0 (highly corrupt). Table 3.12 shows that Nigeria ranks 147th (out of 180 countries), close to Indonesia and better than Kenya and Venezuela. Moreover, it is important to note that fewer firms in Nigeria perceive corruption to be a major or very severe constraint to business when compared to firms in Kenya, República Bolivariana de Venezuela, and Indonesia, the *Nigeria 2008—Enterprise Surveys* show. Thus, while corruption remains a very serious problem in Nigeria, the abysmal image Nigeria has internationally may not be entirely justified when the statistics are considered.

It could be argued that managers have grown to accept corruption and hence report a lower level of corruption even though the problem is actually higher than perceived. To address this concern, more objective indicators of corruption can be examined, such as the amount of bribes paid "to get things done." Even in this case, the amount of bribes paid by firms in Nigeria is lower than what is paid in Kenya and similar to the amount paid in Indonesia (figure 3.3). Furthermore, looking at the evolution of corruption over time, in the last few years Nigeria's corruption level has been improving (figure 3.14). This finding is confirmed by other sources and is a result of the significant effort taken by the Nigerian government to fight corruption through the enacting of the Corrupt Practices and Other Related Offences Act and the establishment of the Independent

Table 3.12   Corruption Perceptions Index, 2007

Country	Rank (180 countries)	Index
Nigeria	147	2.2
Kenya	150	2.1
Venezuela, R.B. de	162	2.0
Brazil	72	3.5
Indonesia	143	2.3
South Africa	43	5.1
India	72	3.5
China	72	3.5

Source: Transparency International.

Figure 3.14   Evolution of Nigeria's Percentile Rank for Rule of Law, Control of Corruption

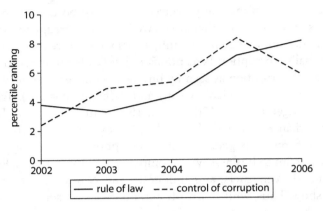

Source: World Bank Governance Indicators 2008.

Corrupt Practices and Other Related Offences Commission (ICPC), as well as the Economic and Financial Crimes Commission. Transparency International's Global Corruption Barometer (2007) would seem to confirm this assessment.[4]

Crime was reported to be a serious constraint to business by 23 percent of firms. However, crime generates indirect costs of only 0.8 percent of sales, which is lower than those associated with electricity outages or even corruption. According to the *Nigeria 2008—Enterprise Surveys*, 20 percent of firms in the formal sector experienced losses as a result of theft, robbery, vandalism, or arson. In an international comparison, with the exception of India, crime is perceived to be a more serious constraint everywhere else than in Nigeria, although it generates more or less similar indirect costs as in Nigeria (figure 3.3).

A side effect of crime is yet another direct cost that would otherwise not be borne by firms: security. In Nigeria, almost 70 percent of firms have to pay for security services, and spend on average 1.8 percent of their annual sales for such services. Large firms appear to bear higher security costs than small and medium firms (table 3.13). In an international comparison, while the share of firms that use security services is similar across countries (except for Indonesia and China), the overall cost burden of security services paid by Nigerian firms is among the highest (table 3.14). While crime is not in the group of the most important constraints, it remains a significant obstacle to doing business in Nigeria due to its considerable cost implications.

Table 3.13 Security Services and Security Expenditures—All Formal Sectors

	TOTAL	Firm size			Ownership		Industry			State	
		Small	Med.	Large	Foreign	Dom.	Manuf.	Retail	Other	More industrialized	Less industrialized
Percentage of firms that paid for security services	**69**	65	84	100	100	69	72	66	68	72	65
Security cost as % annual sales	**1.8**	1.8	1.8	2.6	2.6	1.8	2.1	1.3	1.9	1.8	1.9

Source: Nigeria 2008—Enterprise Surveys.

Table 3.14   Formal Security Services and Security Expenditures—Country Comparisons

	Nigeria 2006	Kenya 2007	Venezuela, R.B. de 2006	Brazil 2003	Indonesia 2003	South Africa 2003	India 2005	China 2002
Percentage of firms that paid for security services	69	70	75	81	46	81	66	48
Security cost as % annual sales	1.8	1.9	6.6	1.6	1.1	0.9	1.3	0.7

Source: Nigeria 2008—Enterprise Surveys.

Summary: Nigeria's Business Environment for the Knowledge Economy

A conducive business environment is required for firms to take advantage of knowledge opportunities. Nigeria has been slipping on the Knowledge Economy Index largely due to the slow improvement in creating an enabling environment for business. The *Doing Business 2010* ranking has seen Nigeria falling by five places compared to the previous year. This is a clear signal that a reversal is needed and will be essential if Nigeria is to aspire to move forward from its factor-driven stage of development into a knowledge-driven economy in the future.

A more supportive business environment will help attract FDI in sectors other than oil and gas or telecom, which have received the lion's share of FDI over the past five years. In this way, Nigeria will be better able to tap into the wealth of knowledge that multinational companies often bring. By fostering business linkages with local SMEs, better production systems and superior technology could be passed on to local firms, thereby increasing their productivity and international competitiveness. Given the large untapped resources Nigeria has— from fertile, uncultivated land to a large, young population, which can be both a production tool and a huge market—international investors' interest is likely to be very large, provided the conditions are in place for them to feel their money will get the expected returns.

A supportive regulatory environment must also be present for innovations to spread and take root. In this context, a tricky trade-off exists between the need to foster the respect of international property rights (IPRs), in order not to alienate potentially interested investors and innovators willing to set up shop in the country, and that of tapping into knowledge and discoveries created elsewhere and applying reverse engineering techniques to foster innovation in Nigeria. The latter method has been used notoriously in several countries, including some of the most successful emerging economies, e.g., Korea, China, and India. Nigeria will have to be very careful in striking a balance between the tempting "copy and adapt" technique and the need to respect international laws and avoid being shunned by international investors.

Access to finance for firms will also be essential to fulfill Nigeria's aspirations for 2020. Business start-up and expansion will need support through the provision of tailored credit products by the financial sector. Business development services will also be key to improving firms' access to formal finance. While the ratio of private credit to GDP is growing at an annualized rate of 72 percent (Isern et al. 2009), outreach of financial services to entrepreneurs, particularly for SMEs, remains limited. Most credit from the banking sector flows into larger corporate entities or multinational companies, with some exceptions being made for smaller contractors operating in the oil and gas or telecom sectors.

The adoption of innovation and know-how is needed at the SME level. SMEs do not often benefit from strong linkages with multinational corporations in the country or from the exchange of know-how and technologies with the outside world through export activities. In a vicious circle, their inability to tap into these sources of knowledge makes them less competitive in international markets and incapable of performing to the standards (in terms of quality, price, product specifications, production time, etc.) required by foreign markets or large corporations present in Nigeria.

Over the past few years, the government has made strides in improving foreign investors' confidence in the Nigerian business environment, for example, by setting up the a "one-stop shop" at the Nigerian Investment Promotion Commission to make investment easier in the country and by fostering more transparent bidding processes for resources and contracts. However, the recent renegotiation of tax clauses in contracts by the federal government with some of the major oil companies does not give the kind of signal foreign investors are seeking. A more conducive business environment, with well-defined, noncontradictory rules, would prove very helpful for the country to tap into the growing stock of global knowledge that foreign companies possess. This could be complemented with strategic alliances between such companies and the federal and state governments in an effort to attract international market players willing to transfer knowledge to local partners, for example by encouraging local content requirements.

Notes

1. The *Nigeria 2008—Enterprise Surveys* is a survey of firms in the manufacturing sector. Considering the exposure of Nigerian banks, most credit goes to the oil and gas (26 percent) and telecom (24 percent) sectors (JP Morgan 2007).

2. However, smaller loans also require some form of collateral as per market practice (Isern et al. 2009).

3. It grew by 6.4 percent in 2008 and close to 6.5 percent per annum in the five-year period since 2004, according to the Central Bank of Nigeria.

4. Respondents to the survey in Nigeria seem broadly optimistic and expect corruption to become less of a problem in the future. They also consider the government's efforts to fight corruption to be effective.

CHAPTER 4

Expanding Nigeria's Information Infrastructure

Information Infrastructure is Key to Productivity and Economic Growth

In today's knowledge-based world, information and communication technology (ICT) plays an increasingly central role in economic growth and productivity. Recent evidence has shown that an increase of 10 mobile phones per 100 people can boost GDP growth by 0.6 percent and a 1 percent increase in the number of Internet users can increase total exports by 4.3 percent (National Media 2007). Rapid advances in information infrastructure are dramatically affecting the acquisition, creation, dissemination, and use of knowledge, which in turn affects economic and social activities, including how manufacturers, service providers, and governments are organized, and how they perform their functions. To develop a strong information infrastructure, it is necessary to mobilize the many stakeholders involved in its deployment and use: the telecommunications networks, strategic information systems, policy and legal frameworks, and skilled human resources needed to use and develop the sector.

Experience shows that a competitive ICT sector is a prerequisite for improving information infrastructure. Creating a competitive environment is one of the defining factors in a country's ability to embrace the knowledge economy. Improving a country's telecom infrastructure will

Figure 4.1   Nigeria's ICT Infrastructure Fails to Keep Pace with Global Improvements

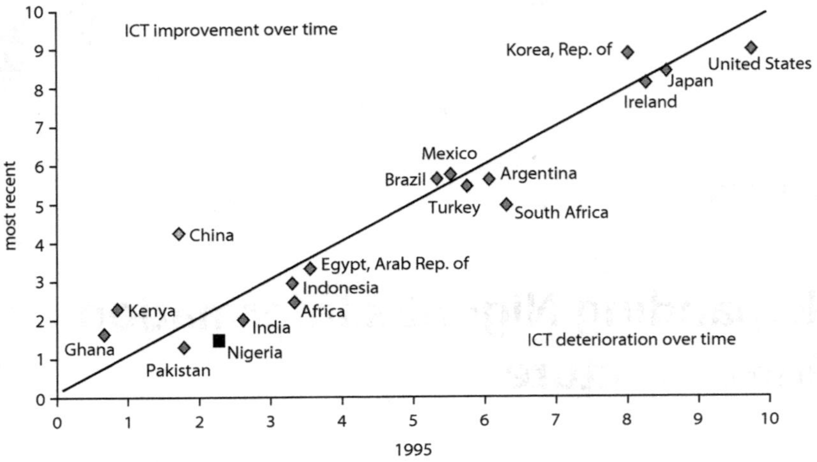

Source: World Bank Knowledge Assessment Methodology 2009.

not only help increase ICT literacy levels, but will also support sustained economic growth. In this regard Nigeria is slipping in relation to the rest of the world, as figure 4.1 shows.

Benchmarking Nigeria's Information Infrastructure

Explosive Telecom Sector Growth

The accelerated liberalization of the past decade has allowed the rapid growth of Nigeria's ICT sector. A telecom penetration rate of more than 32 percent has been reached (up from 2 percent in 2002 and above the regional average of 27 percent), with a mobile footprint covering most of the country. In the process, the telecom sector has attracted more than US$12 billion worth of investment and is contributing more than 2 percent of GDP (up from 0.37 percent in 1999). This, combined with a burgeoning local IT industry and a prolific film industry—estimated at about US$250 million in 2008 (Vanguard 2008), has contributed to providing employment for more than 3.5 million Nigerians, putting the country on the global map for ICT/IT business.

Nigeria's telecom market generated about US$7.5 billion in service revenue in 2006 (Pyramid Research 2007) and is poised to overtake

South Africa as the largest telecommunications market in Africa. The sector is registering a remarkable average growth rate of about 31 percent per annum, the highest of any non-oil sector in the country. The total number of subscribers increased from about 2.3 million to more than 60 million between 2002 and 2008 (Nigeria Communications Commission Web site 2008). As figure 4.2 indicates, this is one of the fastest growth rates in the world.

Most of this growth is attributed to the exceptionally strong development of the mobile telephone sector (37 percent growth rate in 2007) (Business Monitor International 2008), which accounts for more than 95 percent of the Nigerian market and about 20 percent of the African market. The growth is primarily the result of market liberalization, with four national Global System for Mobile communications (GSM) mobile operators, two fixed telecom operators, and a number of private telecom operators using a fixed-wireless technology called CDMA.[1] The recent award of four 3rd Generation (3G) licenses for high-speed mobile data services, the introduction of a unified licensing regime,[2] and continued deployment of CDMA-based services, are likely to further increase competitiveness in the environment as well as provide an opportunity for both fixed and mobile operators to increase the scope of their licenses. Like most African countries, however, Nigeria's fixed telecommunications market has performed far below that of the mobile sector (figure 4.3). The

Figure 4.2   Explosive Growth in Nigerian Telecom Sector

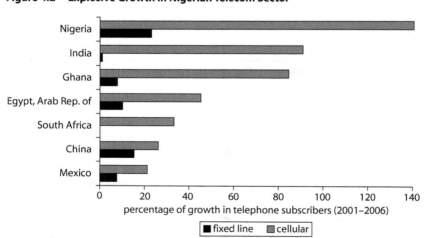

percentage of growth in telephone subscribers (2001–2006)

■ fixed line   ■ cellular

Source: International Telecommunications Union 2008.

Figure 4.3   Nigeria's Telecom Sector Dominated by Mobile Segment

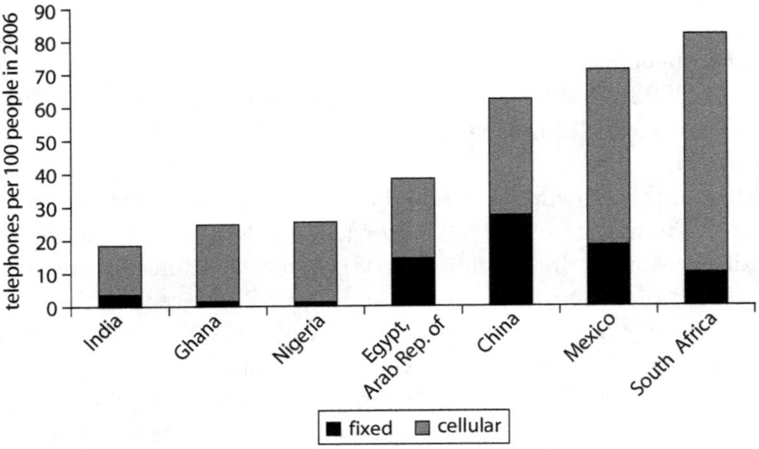

Source: International Telecommunications Union 2008.

Table 4.1   Mobile Prices Fall but Still High

Countries	Connection Charge (US$)	Mobile: Per-minute Local Calls (US$)	
		Peak	Off-Peak
Tanzania	0.2	0.26	0.22
Ghana	1.6	0.15	0.11
Côte d'Ivoire	2.1	0.28	0.28
Uganda	2.9	0.28	0.20
Nigeria	3.0	0.34	0.30
Senegal	5.2	0.26	0.22
SSA Average	10.2	0.30	0.24

Source: International Telecommunications Union 2008 and Nigerian Communications Commission 2008.

number of fixed lines as of March 2008 was approximately 2.5 million, 80 percent of which are being provided by the new private telecom operators using fixed wireless technologies.

An increasingly competitive environment is driving down prices for telecom services in Nigeria (table 4.1). The average per-minute cost of domestic prepaid mobile (at peak times) has declined from about US$0.41 to US$0.34 between 2003 and 2008, but still remains well above the region's average of about US$0.24.

Internet Penetration Continues to Grow but Remains Low

Internet penetration and usage in Nigeria continues to grow, although at a much slower pace than voice services. The number of Internet users stood at about 8 million in December 2007, representing a penetration rate of about 5.3 percent (up from 2.2 million in 2005). While the household penetration is low, most of the large towns and cities have Internet cafes that service much larger populations.

The Internet market is plagued by poor network quality and sluggish rollout, as well as low fixed line and personal computer (PC) penetration. This is further compounded by the lack of a robust national fiber backbone for trunk transmission. NITEL, the incumbent fixed telecom operator, operates its own national switching network system consisting of secondary, primary, and local exchanges, several satellite gateways, and a long-distance transport network. However, very few of its more than 400,000 lines are connected to homes outside of the urban areas, while approximately 60 percent of Nigeria's population lives in rural areas. The country continues to face an inadequate supply of more and better ICT services for Nigeria's 143 million people, as well as significant gaps in key market segments, especially Internet (figure 4.4). Mobile Internet access is increasingly becoming the service of choice for most business and residential customers, but prices are still very high (figure 4.5).

Figure 4.4   Internet Usage per 100 People, 2006

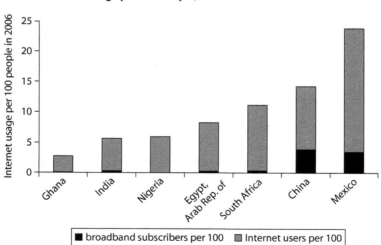

Source: International Telecommunications Union 2008.

Figure 4.5   Nigeria's Communications Prices Remain High

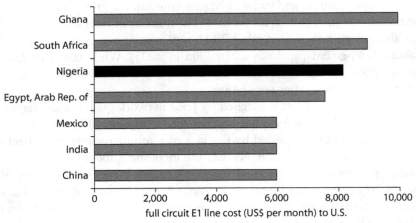

full circuit E1 line cost (US$ per month) to U.S.

Source: International Telecommunications Union 2008.

The lack of a fiber network with national coverage in Nigeria may have more significant implications for the data market than for the voice market. Only about 200,000 of the 8 million Internet subscribers are thought to be using broadband connections. Large data customers typically require large volumes of capacity, high quality, and low prices, which can only be provided on fiber-based transmission networks. Without this, large data users are reliant on wireless technologies, which often have technical and economic limitations. The absence of high-quality transmission capacity on a fiber network within Nigeria is thus constraining the development of data services and the industries that are heavy users of data services—in particular, the IT and IT-enabled industries, as well as e-government applications (figure 4.6).

International Communications
NITEL's control of the SAT 3 cable further entrenches the relatively high prices of international communications. The SAT 3/WASC cable is a 14,350-kilometer undersea fiber optic cable that runs along the western coast of Africa and connects Africa to Europe and Asia through landing points in nine African countries, including Nigeria. The consortium that owns the cable has also used its monopoly powers to control access to and prices for the cable, thereby contributing to the relatively higher prices in the region.[3]

Figure 4.6   Nigeria Lacks Internet Hosts

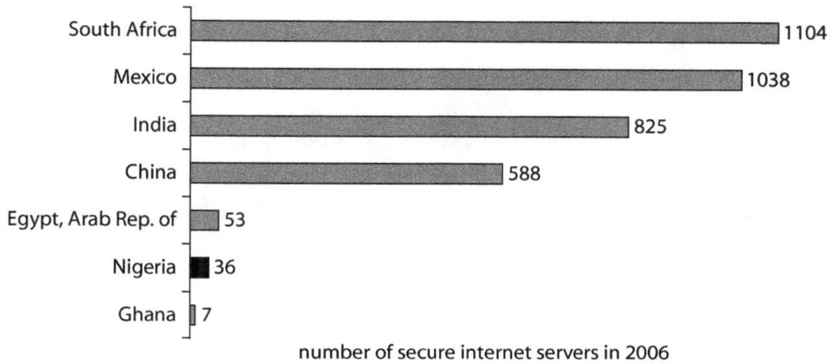

number of secure internet servers in 2006

Source: World Bank 2008.

Nigeria also has three gateway licenses that allow operators to carry voice and data traffic in and out of Nigeria. These operators—NITEL, Globacom, and Prest Cable & Satellite TV—use their international gateways to carry outgoing call traffic from their own customers as well as others. In addition, mobile operators are licensed to send and receive international traffic (albeit only to and from their own customers).

High prices and low capacity have implications for economic growth. The combined impact of inadequate and high-priced domestic and international capacity, and the pervasive lack of power supply that affects telecommunication operations, have implications for economic growth in Nigeria. This is particularly true for the IT and IT-enabled service sector, as well as for use of IT to improve government services. The situation is likely to improve with the launch of the Globacom submarine cable, which is expected to compete with the SAT 3. In addition, the Nigeria Communications Commission's (NCC) plans to increase investment in the sector through public-private partnership (PPP) initiatives, such as the Wire Nigeria Project[4] and the State Accelerated Broadband Initiative.[5]

Policy and Regulatory Environment

Recent Nigerian administrations have championed an aggressive telecom reform program by opening the sector to new competitors and establishing a modern regulatory framework. The adoption of the Nigerian Communications Act of 2003 has strengthened the NCC's enforcement powers and provided considerable independence from the Ministry of Information and Communications. The NCC has been quite effective in developing one of the most competitive telecom sectors in Africa. The commission has been rated second (after Uganda) as the most independent and first in business environment rankings among 20 African countries surveyed in 2008 (Business Monitor International 2008).

Efforts to deepen competition have included full liberalization of the local and mobile segments, and partial liberalization of domestic and international long-distance service. The results of the open and competitive regulatory framework are quite evident, with more than US$12 billion of investment to date, according to the NCC, and about US$7.5 billion in service revenues for 2006 alone. The sector has been able to attract most of the leading regional players into the country. The current administration is continuing the reform effort and has urged the NCC to address the overstretched network capacity and the poor service quality. Pressure from the parliamentary committee for the NCC and the Ministry of Information and Communication to institute more effective measures, including better planning and controls to improve network and service quality, is forcing all of the major operators to invest heavily in network expansion.

In the meantime, the combined impact of unprecedented growth and the increasingly competitive environment continues to challenge the NCC's capacity to proactively manage the enforcement of network and service quality standards. A multitude of licenses have been issued by NCC in the past five years to meet the growing demand for services, and the lack of clarity between the mandates of the NCC and the Nigerian Broadcast Commission regarding spectrum issues continues to be a problem for the sector. Efforts to merge the two institutions have yet to be finalized.

Summary: Nigeria's ICT Infrastructure

A good ICT backbone is an absolute requisite for a functioning knowledge economy. Nigerians need to be able to communicate with one another and access the Internet for business purposes. Nowadays, the Internet provides access to almost the entire spectrum of human knowledge, but it is also a conduit for business services and a channel to market for Nigeria's software developers and other IT-enabled services.

Nigeria has made rapid strides in expanding telecom access in recent years, but these successes are largely confined to the mobile telephony space. Access to landlines has deteriorated and Internet access remains costly, with bandwidth severely limited. The country can learn from its

Figure 4.7   How Nigeria Stands in Relation to African Competitors

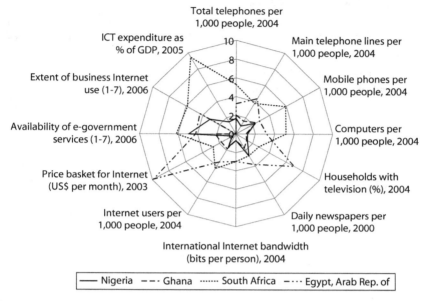

Source: World Bank Knowledge Assessment Methodology 2009.

success in mobile telephony and put in place a business environment that will foster competition, which will in turn galvanize the private sector to provide high-quality services at reasonable costs.

Only when bandwidth is increased and its cost reduced will the stage be set for all other areas, such as e-government, computer ownership, and Internet usage, to flourish. The federal government can promote this evolution by increasing ICT spending, promoting e-government services, subsidizing IT training within the government, and promoting ICT literacy in Nigerian schools. Figure 4.7 highlights how Nigeria stands in relation to its competitors in terms of its information infrastructure.

Notes

1. This allows them to offer "limited mobility" as well as higher speed for data services than basic mobile technologies.

2. This move is consistent with the global regulatory trend toward unified license regimes that allow fixed operators to provide mobile services and vice versa.

3. These remain lower than prices in the eastern part of Africa, where the installation of an undersea cable has not been completed.

4. The Wire Nigeria project is expected to include a comprehensive national fiber optic backbone network to ensure that all Nigerians are within 50 kilometers of a fiber network.

5. The State Accelerated Broadband Initiative is expected to improve affordable broadband access throughout the country.

CHAPTER 5

Creating an Innovation Culture

What Is an Innovation System?

A country's innovation system is the set of institutions, procedures, and processes that determine how it can create, acquire, disseminate, and use knowledge and information. In practice, this is the network of universities, research centers, think tanks, firms, business associations, and, more generally, producers and users of knowledge in the country. This system can support or hinder the interaction between global and local sources of knowledge and the assimilation of the growing stock of global knowledge.

A forward-looking innovation system that supports qualitative knowledge interaction among various parties is critical for building a knowledge economy. In this context, innovation as a concept must be intended not just as the domestic development of cutting-edge scientific discoveries, but also as the adaptation and use of existing knowledge in the local context. As Utz (2006) asserts: "Innovation in the context of developing countries thus needs to be understood in a broad way: it consists of the design, development, and diffusion of a technology (or a practice) which is new for the society concerned."

Many developing countries have a long way to go before they can start creating new technologies. This does not mean that their development should not focus on creating an innovation culture. The largest rewards from technology do not accrue to those that invent new technologies but to those that adopt them, adapt them, and make them practical in their local context. This is often overlooked by many countries when they embark on farsighted development strategies that include a focus on technology. Thus, an innovation culture for developing countries must be understood as the building of a technical culture and a system of incentives that support the adoption and, subsequently the adaptation, of existing (often foreign) technologies (Utz 2006). Several studies have shown that developing countries reap far greater dividends by simply accessing and adopting existing technologies than inventing new ones. The success of the East Asian economies has also followed this pattern of first moving to existing best practices and then attempting to develop new technologies.

The innovation process can be broken down into three key steps, which generally follow the process of development of the country concerned:

1. Local adoption of existing technologies
2. Adaptation of existing technologies to the local context and their use for the development of competitive industries
3. Development of new technologies in the country

Nigeria is at the "factor-driven" stage of development, according to Michael Porter's stages of national competitive development. Developing countries at this stage tend to rely mainly on things such as natural resources and unskilled labor, while seeking to move to the "investment-driven" stage, where the transfer of technology and investment in human and physical capital allows them to prepare the ground for the "innovation" stage—the knowledge-driven economy (Porter 1991). Progress in Nigeria's quest for building a knowledge economy can be measured and benchmarked through the KAM Database.

Benchmarking Nigeria's Innovation System

Nigeria's innovation system has been holding its ground since 1995. Figure 5.1 depicts the improvement registered on the KAM's Innovation Index for a number of countries. Countries above the line are those that have improved the performance of their innovation system between 1995 and the most recent measurement undertaken, relative to other countries. Nigeria rests right on the line, while peers like Ghana, Egypt, and South Africa have seen their positions slightly worsen over the past decade.

Figure 5.1   World Innovation Improvements since 1995

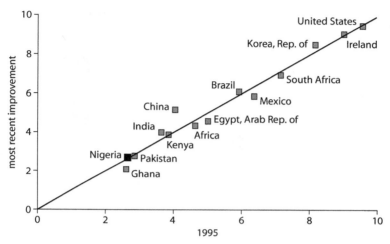

Source: World Bank Knowledge Assessment Methodology 2009.

Rather predictably, key emerging markets like India and China have been making progress.

However, in absolute terms, Nigeria's innovation system is still less advanced than those of the chosen comparator countries, particularly South Africa (figure 5.2). Despite being largely on par with Ghana, Nigeria scores well below Egypt and South Africa, especially on firm-level technology absorption; private sector overall spending on R&D; patents obtained; scientific articles published; and university/private company cooperation. Nigeria beats its southern rival only in terms of FDI inflows as a percentage of GDP, and most of this is explained in terms of the huge inflows of foreign investment into the oil and gas and communication sectors over the past few years.

Nigeria needs to strengthen collaboration between universities and the private sector. In this area, Nigeria seems to be on a par with Ghana, Egypt, and Mexico, but lags behind China, South Africa, and India (figure 5.3). In India, for example, strong linkages exist among the private sector, tertiary education institutions, and research bodies, such as the Indian Institutes of Technology (IITs) and the Indian Institutes of Management (IIMs), which also have close ties with leading foreign universities and research institutes (Wijesinha 2008). Such linkages have supported knowledge dissemination and transfer to the real sector of the economy.

Figure 5.2   Promising Path to Be Supported in Cooperation with the Private Sector

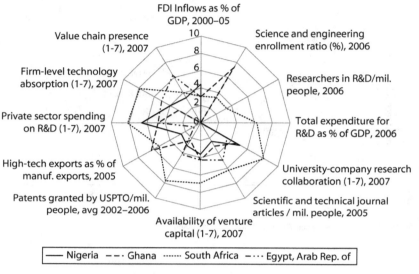

Cross-country comparison of innovation parameters

Source: World Bank Knowledge Assessment Methodology 2009.

Figure 5.3   Weak Linkages between Universities and Businesses

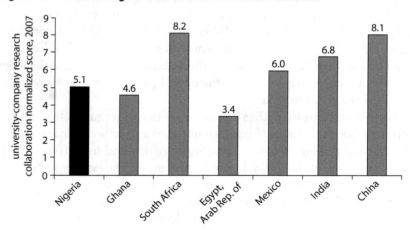

Source: World Bank Knowledge Assessment Methodology 2009.
Note: Variables normalized from 0 (weakest) to 10 (strongest). The same is true for the figures following.

Few patents are granted to Nigerian companies. Figure 5.4 indicates that the number of patents granted by the USPTO to Nigeria is lower than for most comparator countries, demonstrating the low level of sophistication of scientific research in the country. This is due to decades of underinvestment and waste in the education sector, which particularly suffered during the repressive military regimes, as well as to the flight of talent experienced during the 1990s.[1] The limited resources of research institutes and the problems that beset Nigeria's reputation in the international press have also contributed over the years to a certain degree of isolation of the country from major international centers of knowledge production and application. With the return to democracy and an increasing number of Nigerians in the Diaspora making their way back home, this trend could be reversed, provided a concerted effort is put forth by the government. A good example is Malaysia's drive to track and attract back its expatriates who have graduated from top international universities. Many Nigerians are starting to return and government can continue to ensure that they are empowered to play a positive role in the nation's economic development. Making it easier for foreigners to live and work in Nigeria can also serve to bring much needed managerial and technical talent to the country. In this area Malaysia has been a leader through the "Malaysia My Second Home" program, which has allowed foreigners to invest in real estate in the country and gain permanent resident status.

Firm-level capacity to absorb technology in Nigeria is weak. This is a key area in which a knowledge economy can outperform a traditional economy.

Figure 5.4   Low Levels of Sophistication in Scientific Research

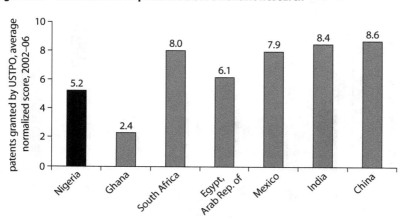

Source: World Bank Knowledge Assessment Methodology 2009.

Firm-level productivity is the main driver behind competitiveness and economic growth. The World Bank Investment Climate Assessment showed that most firms in Nigeria are poorly managed and few have adopted leading-edge technologies. This relatively poor performance is also an opportunity as it hints at the massive gains that are possible with improved technology absorption and deployment (figure 5.5).

In an international comparison, India leads the group in innovation, with the boom in the IT sector and the "outsourcing" phenomenon. With its educated, English-speaking population ready to work at very competitive wages, it has created a second "Silicon Valley" manned by a growing number of trained engineers and technicians and powered by strong cooperation between colleges and IT firms. A similar process has started in China, where the global outsourcing industry has been gradually moving and where other forms of technology adoption by firms have supported the impressively high growth rates experienced by the country in recent years in all areas of manufacturing, from cheaper versions of clothing to IT software and assembled components. Nigeria, with its English-speaking population and cheap labor, can closely study the development path of these new international giants and identify areas in which it needs to focus to become competitive (e.g., a better quality education system closely tied to market needs). It can also learn from some of their mistakes.

Nigerian private sector spending on R&D compares well with peer countries. Although Nigeria still lags behind key emerging markets, the statistics illustrate that the Nigerian private sector demonstrates interest

Figure 5.5   Missing an Opportunity to Innovate

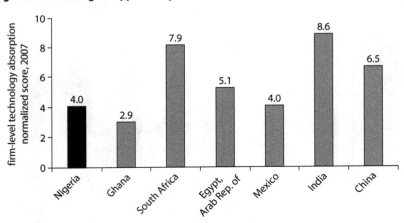

Source: World Bank Knowledge Assessment Methodology 2009.

and commitment to innovation, possibly spurred by the low levels of government funding (figure 5.6). However, anecdotal evidence seems to contrast with this picture. Given the high protectionism that characterized the Nigerian trade system until recently,[2] and the high concentration levels in certain market segments (both in goods and services), Nigerian firms have not had big incentives to innovate, as they could reap large profits protected behind high tariff walls, regardless of their R&D expenditures. This situation now seems to be changing. Although the spending recorded is possibly still at the stage of local adaptation and internalization of know-how produced and tested outside the country, it represents an excellent springboard from which to launch Nigeria into the knowledge economy. Although it has a long way to go when compared to South Africa, India, and China, Nigeria is in a good position to start developing original technology and know-how in the near future.

From the data available, it appears that the Nigerian innovation system has performed relatively well and maintained a stable ranking over the past decade. However, if Nigeria is to achieve its vision to become one of the top 20 economies by 2020 (Vision 2020), it must make innovation the center of its development strategy going forward.

Much can be done to improve the innovation culture across Nigerian society. This can start by devoting adequate resources to encourage innovation. Government could boost support to R&D by increasing funding to the significant number of underfunded Nigerian research institutions. Ideally, this would be achieved in tandem with a restructuring of these

Figure 5.6   Nigeria's Private Sector Leads Way to Innovation

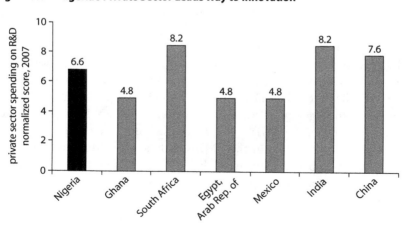

Source: World Bank Knowledge Assessment Methodology 2009.

institutes to encourage partnerships with the private sector and additional fund raising from remunerated activities. Many of the existing institutes are weakly linked to the private sector because of a lack of financial resources and partnership agreements, which make them unable to achieve their potential in terms of contributing to the country's innovation system.

Extracting a few key priorities from the new national strategy on science and technology could provide a sound framework for innovation in the country and support the realization of the president's seven-point agenda, e.g., in supporting the diversification of the real sector and delivering higher agricultural production for food security. The policy, revised in 2006 with assistance from UNESCO, rightly puts emphasis on science as a fundamental part of any Nigerian child's education and on some key areas that the country should focus on, such as ICT, agriculture, and biotechnological research. It is important to start with manageable projects to avoid overstretching or wasting scarce resources, as in the case of the US$311 million Nigerian Communications Satellite (NIGCOMSAT-1), which was launched in 2007 and disappeared in 2008.[3]

Business associations could play a useful role in the transfer of knowledge. Nigeria should focus on fostering its innovation culture by adoption and adaptation to the local context of existing technologies. In this context, a major role could be played by the myriad of business associations across the country: NACCIMA (the Nigerian Association of Chambers of Commerce, Industry, Mines, and Agriculture), MAN (the Manufacturers Association of Nigeria), etc., as well as the Nigerian Diaspora. They could help information flow from sources within and outside the country to their members on knowledge, innovations, prices, quality standards, etc.

Increasing opportunities for the diffusion of know-how and technical knowledge via the provision of business development services (BDS) would also foster the adoption of new production systems and more advanced technology by local firms. Several business associations, public (e.g., SMEDAN or the Small and Medium Enterprise Development Agency of Nigeria, and private (e.g., NACCIMA) alike, provide their members with such services. Commercial banks, looking into expanding business in the SME sector, are also starting BDS programs, often in partnership with donors, e.g., Diamond Bank and the International Finance Corporation. This new and welcome trend must be strengthened with adequate financial and technical support from both the government and the private sector, and could be a viable field for the promotion of public-private partnerships, encompassing universities, local consultancy companies, businesses, and the donor community.

In-firm training is another way of spreading knowledge and know-how. At present, only 26 percent of Nigerian firms provide training to their workers (Iarossi et al. 2008). These tend to be the largest, exporting, or foreign-owned firms. Nonetheless, Iarossi et al. (2008) find that, once firm size is controlled for, training does not have an independent effect on value added per worker. This is because the training provided in Nigerian firms is often theoretical or obsolete and does not equip workers with the necessary tools to positively impact the productivity of their firms. Not only is there a strong need to increase in-firm training, there is also the need to improve its quality and ensure that applicable, practical know-how is transferred.

Stronger regional integration through ECOWAS could support the innovation effort and produce positive cross-country spillovers. Nigeria is the "giant" of the ECOWAS community. As such it has extraordinary opportunities as well as responsibilities in pushing the innovation agenda forward in the subregion. By leveraging on its economic and political influence, it could support regional initiatives aimed at productive exchanges of information and knowledge (e.g., from foreign language learning, which is still a barrier to integration in ECOWAS, to profitable trade exchanges of raw materials, managerial know-how, and other inputs). The establishment of an oil pipeline that will serve several countries in the subregion and the adoption of a new, harmonized system of trade tariffs, represent very encouraging steps toward regional integration and the basis for other key projects and exchanges in the future (ICT infrastructure, school exchange programs, etc.), which could support the spread of ideas and know-how throughout the subregion.

The Diaspora could become the driving force behind Nigeria's knowledge economy efforts. It is calculated that more than 15 million Nigerians live outside of the country (Nworah 2005). Among them are accomplished physicians, scientists, businessmen, economists, writers, and artists. All of them, and particularly those in science and business, have a tremendous amount of know-how to offer. By transferring the practical knowledge of production systems (from supply chain management to knowledge management software, etc.), international standards, regulations, and markets, they could foster innovation in their homeland to a great extent. In this effort, they would possess a comparative advantage that stems from their unique understanding of the local context, of cultural and business practices, and of specific constraints. In this way, they could facilitate the implementation of the "adopt-and-adapt" strategy as the basis of Nigeria's knowledge economy (box 5.1).

Finally, industrial clusters can facilitate knowledge and innovation sharing. Clusters have the potential to improve firms' competitiveness by

---

Box 5.1

Nigerian Brain Drain

Brain drain is a phenomenon that unfortunately is common in the whole of Africa. Nigeria has been hit particularly hard and has lost a critical mass that now staffs the hospitals, universities, and firms of Europe and the United States. In the past, the country lost much of its talent because of its inability to remunerate it, to offer interesting economic opportunities, to maintain linkages with centers of excellence abroad, and to provide good quality education. During the years of military dictatorships, spending cuts in education, and stagnant economic growth, many educated Nigerians moved abroad, where they are now esteemed professionals in their fields. The problem intensified over the 1990s because of the particularly repressive political regimes in place and the intensification of globalization with the accompanied reduced cost of international movement. Former President Babangida's "Presidential Committee on Brain Drain," set up in 1988, calculated that Nigeria lost more than 10,000 academics from tertiary institutions alone between 1986 and 1990. Considering those who left public and private organizations of all types, the count rises to 30,000, according to the UN Economic Commission for Africa.

Lately, with the return of democracy and the boost in economic growth, there has been a slight reversal, with some Nigerians being attracted by the new opportunities springing up in their homeland. The African Diaspora Initiative, which works with the Nigerian government to encourage returns, estimates that 7,500 Nigerians have come back to work in the financial, telecom, and IT industries in the past seven years. Some "returnees" are high-profile individuals and have been chosen for high-level positions in government and industry, but many more have returned to take up positions mainly in the civil service in Abuja, in banks in Lagos, and in oil companies in Port Harcourt. Many others have started investing more heavily back home and creating new firms. The private sector has also been recruiting aggressively among Nigerians in the Diaspora, offering competitive compensation packages to lure talent into coming home, e.g., commercial banks recruiting in the City of London.

(continued)

Box 5.1 *(Continued)*

These rather spontaneous examples should be encouraged through concerted actions, sponsored in partnership by the government and the private sector, to attract the large pool of Nigerians abroad who need to be convinced that is worth their while to leave their established careers and living standards abroad to return home. Among these potential actions are:

- Recruiting Nigerians from abroad for permanent positions or through technical assistance schemes, which provide adequate compensation and career prospects
- Improving employment opportunities in Nigeria through private sector-led growth and the professionalization of the civil service, reforming the latter to support meritocracy and offer competitive salary packages
- Raising the standards in local universities and research centers to attract back the Diaspora from foreign centers of learning, and from private companies willing to set up shop in Nigeria to exploit the newly created pool of talent
- Encouraging cooperation in education (e.g., from exchanges to foreign language learning) and investment promotion in the West African subregion, through ECOWAS, for the spread of indigenous knowledge and know-how.

Sources: Utz 2006, UN Economic Commission for Africa, Financial Times 2009.

driving innovation, given the accumulation of a critical mass of players that can generate and disseminate sector-specific knowledge (Porter 1990). In this context, the World Bank has been supporting the government of Nigeria through the identification of "growth poles" to encourage the formation of such clusters, along the lines of successful projects carried out in other countries.

Summary: Creating an Innovation Culture

By leveraging its endowment of resources and its population's renowned entrepreneurial spirit and belief in the private sector, Nigeria can go a long way to foster an innovation culture. Refocusing priorities and carefully choosing a menu of actions that foster knowledge, technology adoption, and adaptation would help the country target the key building blocks for the development of a solid knowledge economy, which would later entail the local production of new ideas.

Nigeria already has what it takes to create an innovation culture. It has a national strategy on science and technology that could be further revised to provide a sound framework for innovation in the country. A number of business associations already connect members in a diverse and large country and could become key vehicles for knowledge transfer. Such associations could also play a key role in the provision of training and BDS to firms in order to foster the adoption of new production systems, or in the creation of industrial clusters through PPPs. By leveraging its prominent position in ECOWAS and the millions of Nigerians in the Diaspora, Nigeria's innovation culture could receive a boost from the more fluid circulation of tools and ideas.

Notes

1. Legal and illegal immigration of Nigerians to Europe and the United States intensified during the 1990s. (http://www.nigeriandiaspora.com/diaspora.htm)
2. A new harmonized system of ECOWAS tariffs has recently come into effect.
3. The satellite is in the process of being replaced by the company that built it.

PART II

Case Studies

What Can Nigeria Learn from Other Countries?

The second part of this report evaluates the experiences of four other countries in their attempts to make a transition toward the knowledge economy. The case studies involve India, China, Korea, and Singapore; four countries at very different stages in their KE transitions. India, a large country at a similar level of per-capita income as Nigeria, is widely viewed as a leader in offshoring, call centers, and software development. Korea is currently seen as a leader in effectively using knowledge for growth, while Singapore has started pursuing a relatively new strategy in which innovation becomes the focus of the economy. China is in its initial stages of developing a strategy for a knowledge-driven economy.

Nigeria can benefit from observing what has and has not worked for each of these countries. This analysis can offer many insights into how Nigeria can develop its own KE strategy.

CHAPTER 6

India—Creating a Partnership for Knowledge

India's explosive economic growth has propelled it into the realm of the fastest-growing emerging markets. Its GDP has been growing at an average rate of 9 percent a year over the past five years, making it one of the world's largest economies and a major outsourcing hub. India is poised to continue to experience brisk growth rates in the future and become the third-largest economy in terms of GDP, after China and the United States, by 2050 (Goldman Sachs 2007). Even after the setback due to the recent global financial turmoil, growth projections for the country are favorable.

Great untapped potential exists for India to increase productivity, reduce poverty, and fully embark on the knowledge-economy revolution. Following extensive economic reforms begun in 1991 by the then-Finance Minister Manmohan Singh, India has started the move from low-productivity activities in agriculture and the informal sector to more productive and modern ones (Utz and Dahlman 2005), such as IT and pharmaceuticals. The reforms that allowed this transformation need to be pushed forward to enhance the country's productivity and international competitiveness and support India's development into a full-fledged knowledge economy.

India already possesses some of the key ingredients necessary to become a knowledge economy. These include a critical mass of educated,

English-speaking people; top-quality science and technology institutions; macroeconomic stability; one of the world's largest domestic markets; a relatively steady democracy; a vibrant private sector; a large Diaspora; a good ICT infrastructure; and a growing financial sector. Moreover, the government has understood the importance of the knowledge economy agenda and has moved energetically to support it.

In order to become a real knowledge economy, India will have to strengthen its reform process by bringing together the government, the private sector, and civil society (Utz and Dahlman 2005). The economy-wide reforms started in 1991 will have to be deepened. As in Nigeria's case, India still lags on the business environment pillar of the knowledge economy. While the other three pillars (skills and education, ICT infrastructure, and innovation) record a better performance, they are also in need of significant reforms. The real challenge will be to adopt a holistic approach to systematically integrate the changes made in each of these areas, while involving the three key players in the economy—government, the private sector, and civil society.

Where Does India Stand on the Knowledge Economy Today?

India has begun its quest to become a knowledge economy but has some ways to go to catch up with more advanced competitors (figure 6.1). Despite having liberalized its economy, improved its technical and scientific education system, and started an IT revolution, India needs to make more progress to be on a par with other more sophisticated economies. Some, like Korea and Singapore, started their journey toward the knowledge economy much earlier and are now at the innovation-driven stage of economic development. Others, like China, represent the most aggressive competitors of tomorrow, transitioning to the efficiency-driven stage. (World Economic Forum 2009)

India is ranked 35th out of 134 countries for capacity to innovate (World Economic Forum 2009). It has made strides in improving the quality of scientific education and the collaboration between schools and firms and in launching high-skill industries, such as IT and pharmaceuticals. However, it is still lagging behind its comparators and faces important challenges. For example, at current growth rates, India is finding it increasingly difficult to procure the skilled manpower needed to staff its outsourcing industry, especially in view of its expansion into more sophisticated realms, such as financial services and software development. There is also the need to make knowledge available and attainable by a larger

Figure 6.1   India Has a Way to Go to Become a Knowledge Economy

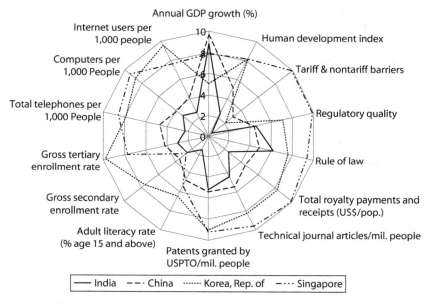

Source: World Bank Knowledge Assessment Methodology 2009.

proportion of the population, as so far the main suppliers of good-quality graduates are a few "elite" colleges.

India also needs to improve its ICT infrastructure and go further in reforming its investment climate. Much of the IT and outsourcing revolution in India has been happening in dedicated ICT parks, which benefit from constant electricity supply and the latest infrastructural developments. Nonetheless, to increase the rate of growth and open the benefits of this boom to a larger share of the population and a wider variety of industries, the existing infrastructure bottlenecks must be tackled. The same is true for institutional barriers, such as difficulties in enforcing contracts, and rigid hiring practices, which stifle competition and discourage firms from investing.

India's Knowledge Economy Strategy

Nonetheless, India has understood the importance of innovation and knowledge for its future and has developed a vision to become a knowledge economy. A series of challenges and opportunities has been identified through a number of strategic papers put together by different organizations, such as India's Planning Commission and the High-Level Strategic Group (Utz and Dahlman 2005).[1] These argue strongly that the fuel of the growth paradigm of the future is "knowledge workers and skilled professionals" (All India Management Association 2003) and warn about the shortage of particular professionals in the future. This could severely hamper economic growth, thus having significant socioeconomic implications, and is particularly important for an emerging market like India, where growth will be essential to lift a large part of the population above the poverty line (All India Management Association 2003). As today's developed countries will face such skill shortages more acutely, India can provide the manpower needed and anchor its success as an offshoring center, provided it commits to becoming a real knowledge economy.

To group and guide all efforts toward developing a knowledge economy strategy, India set up a National Knowledge Commission. The commission[2] is "a high-level advisory body to the Prime Minister of India, with the objective of transforming India into a knowledge society" (National Knowledge Commission 2001). It was established in 2005 with a three-year mandate to empower and enable India's citizens by fostering their ability to use and create knowledge capital and to leverage India's demographic advantage by following a "knowledge-oriented paradigm of development" (National Knowledge Commission 2001). A cornerstone of the commission's philosophy is that "greater participation and more equitable access to knowledge across all sectors of society are of vital importance" (National Knowledge Commission 2001). Hence, the commission aims to strengthen the education system, promoting research and knowledge application to specific industrial sectors; enhance governance by leveraging ICT infrastructure; and devise ways to exchange knowledge globally.

The National Knowledge Commission supported the birth of a strong partnership among government, the private sector, and civil society. Its members include ministries and the Planning Commission. The Planning Commission had total freedom in setting up working groups on different thematic areas. These groups included experts from the private sector and civil society, greatly enhancing the commission's capacity to come up with detailed recommendations on each of the areas it deemed relevant for its knowledge economy strategy (box 6.1).

Despite having identified the key actions, India has not focused on prioritizing them and drawing up a coherent plan. The National Knowledge Commission has produced a set of recommendations for policy makers in

Box 6.1

India's Strategy for a Knowledge Economy

The National Knowledge Commission was charged with the responsibility of drafting a path for India to follow in its quest to develop a "vibrant knowledge-based society." The commission, through working groups, consultations with different stakeholders (universities, state governments, etc.), and surveys, identified the areas that constitute the building blocks of the knowledge economy in the country. These are clustered around five focus areas, namely access, concepts, creation, application, and services, which further break down into 24 subcomponents, ranging from language to higher education, from math and science to international property rights (IPRs), from innovation to entrepreneurship. For each of these areas, the commission developed a set of detailed recommendations to guide policy makers in moving the country forward on its knowledge economy agenda.

Source: www.knowledge commission.gov.in

different subcomponents of the education, innovation, and ICT pillars. It has primarily focused on proposals to boost scientific education, strengthen the ICT infrastructure, and support R&D activities through cross-fertilization of ideas between universities and industry. However, these recommendations have not been put into a sequential strategy with priority actions and phased interventions, and the risk exists that momentum will be lost if too many recommendations in a variety of sectors are put before the government without a thought-out road map.

Moreover, India's knowledge economy agenda has primarily concentrated on the education, ICT, and innovation pillars, paying less attention to the business environment. As Utz and Dahlman (2005) argue, every action taken in the other three pillars will have to be supported by a broad reform agenda that interests the business environment, if the full benefits of the investments undertaken in those three pillars are to be realized. This is "because some elements of India's current economic and institutional regime are constraining the full realization of India's potential" (Utz and Dahlman 2005), due to the lack of an incentive system that encourages the most effective use of resources in those areas.

However, India has realized the importance of strong leadership and a solid partnership among the different players involved in order to move the process forward. The establishment of the National Knowledge

Commission was a great catalyst and a great device to signal the government's intention to focus on the knowledge economy. Reporting directly to the prime minister, the commission was given the ability to involve different knowledge networks and stakeholders and was granted great visibility. The forum it helped in establishing has become a precious tool for advancing this agenda. What India is lacking is a task force or dedicated group to craft a plan of sequenced actions to implement the recommendations put forth by the commission (Utz and Dahlman 2005).

Opportunities and Challenges Facing India's Knowledge Economy

Business Environment

India has come a long way since 1991, becoming a major global player, embracing competition, and opening up to world trade. The country has gained its place among the fastest-growing economies of the world and is projected to overtake Japan and Germany and become the third-largest economy by 2050 (Goldman Sachs 2007). Despite the current global financial crisis, it enjoys a stable macroeconomic outlook, relatively efficient capital markets, an advanced legal system, entrepreneurial people, abundant raw materials, reasonably good infrastructure, a large domestic market, and a comparatively low-cost and skilled labor force.

India has established itself as a major services exporter, especially in IT, becoming a global outsourcing hub. Its ICT services exports have boomed over the past decade and constitute the bulk of its commercial services exports (figure 6.2). This has given rise to knowledge hubs in different areas of the country, e.g., Hyderabad and Bangalore. In these hubs, foreign firms outsource different customer services or even software production. ICT parks have become the preferred way to develop this line of business. They provide dedicated areas where electricity and other developed country amenities come at developing country costs, allow talent to be attracted from across the country; and lure key anchor tenants, such as Microsoft Corporation, Compaq, Intel Corporation, Google, etc., to set up shop.

However, a number of barriers and constraints remain. India remains a relatively closed economy compared to others in the region, thus not benefitting from the knowledge and technology transfer, the pressure on improving production efficiency, and the cheaper inputs that come with trade exchanges or FDI. Distortions affect several product and factor markets, particularly land and labor. Enforcing contracts is at times challenging.

Figure 6.2   Boom in IT Services Exports from India

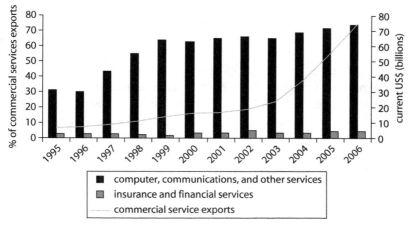

Source: NASSCOM 2007.

Government intervention and business ownership is still significant. Moreover, the vast majority of the population is still employed in less productive agricultural activities, rather than in the manufacturing and service sectors. As a result, a considerable part of the population still lives below the poverty line and income inequality is high.

India should focus on improving its business environment to support its broader knowledge economy agenda. By reducing tariffs and FDI restrictions; simplifying business registration procedures and labor regulations; reforming land laws; enhancing firms' access to finance, reliable power supply, and transport connections; strengthening IPRs; and improving governance, India could help its firms become more competitive and lock in its achievement in becoming a major global service exporter. This would place it in a good position to take on the challenges coming from competing nations, such as China. Moreover, it would back the country's quest toward the knowledge economy by grounding its reforms in the other three pillars on a supportive business environment.

India's Innovation System

India has made tremendous progress in building an innovation system. This has mostly meant introducing modern and efficient practices in a variety of sectors, such as IT and agriculture. The latter has seen diffusion of new knowledge and technology as the basis for the "Green Revolution," which has transformed the country from a net importer into a net exporter of grains (Utz and Dahlman 2005). This has improved the lives of millions of rural poor.

The country has boosted R&D activities, investing in educating its workforce, building the necessary infrastructure, and creating knowledge hubs in different areas of country. More than 100 multinationals operate in India, mainly in different R&D parks, which have supported the creation of powerful alliances between local and international firms, fostering knowledge transfer. A significant venture capital investment market is emerging and the number of new patents granted is increasing (Utz and Dahlman 2005). Linkages have also been established among such hubs, Indian universities, and research institutions, supporting the integration of India among global knowledge players. The high quality of some of these institutions and the workforce operating in them has been key for the outsourcing phenomenon, which is moving more and more toward the high end of the R&D market. From offshore call centers to software developers to financial services providers, India is moving in the right direction to increase the value added and knowledge content of its outsourcing industry in a variety of sectors.

Despite this, India needs to further support its innovation sector if it is to improve its standing as a knowledge economy. A large gap exists between cutting-edge sectors, e.g., IT, pharmaceuticals, etc., and more backward production systems used in others, e.g., textiles. India could support the use of more efficient production processes in the different sectors of the economy by strengthening competition; encouraging trade and FDI; harnessing the knowledge of Indians in the Diaspora; fostering collaborations among multinationals, local firms, and research institutions; boosting funding for R&D through stronger private-sector involvement; leveraging its ability at reverse engineering; and establishing public-private partnerships (Utz and Dahlman 2005).

Growing a Skilled and Educated Workforce

India's education system has made tremendous progress and has been key to its recent IT and technology revolution. Its tertiary institutions include some top-class technology and management institutes, e.g., the Indian Institutes of Technology and the Indian Institutes of Management. India currently produces more than 200,000 scientists, technicians, and engineers per year (Utz and Dahlman 2005). Private-sector funding to education has been on the increase and has contributed to the emergence of these centers of excellence. Nonetheless, it has also brought about more inequality in access to education (Kingdon 2007).[3]

A comprehensive strategy for the education sector is warranted. First, this will have to encourage social inclusion and wider access, possibly through new learning technologies, to build the cadre of educated personnel that Indian industries will need in the future. Currently, the highly skilled workforce is only a tiny fraction of the population and shortages of skilled labor are already predicted in the medium term. The education strategy will have to ensure the quality and relevance of curricula, ensuring the provision of skilled personnel at all levels of production. Thus, vocational training will have to be used to its potential to provide Indian firms with a more flexible workforce. Overall, the education system will have to become more in tune with the needs of the market and be able to provide graduates with the problem-solving and communication skills needed to adapt to a fast-paced production environment that will require constant retraining. Graduates will then have to be provided with appealing opportunities to avoid the brain drain that India has been subject to over the past few decades.

Information Infrastructure
Following liberalizing reforms, India's information infrastructure has been significantly improved. The telecom sector has been growing quickly (figure 6.3), with the introduction of new market players and products and a reduction in service prices. Indian mobile phone services

Figure 6.3   Boom in India's Mobile Telephony

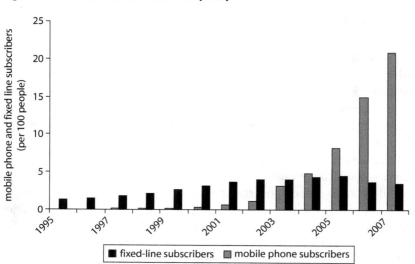

Source: International Telecommunications Union 2008.

are some of the cheapest in the world (Utz and Dahlman 2005). These services have spread to previously isolated areas of the country, boosting economic activity. Broadband Internet connections have also increased in number and coverage. The IT sector has grown 11-fold, moving up the value chain into more complex IT products and consulting services, prompting many IT multinationals to outsource different sections of their production chain to India.

This boom has occurred due to a combination of favorable factors. As mentioned, India has a relatively educated, English-speaking workforce. It produces a considerable number of science and technology graduates from top technical schools and can tap into the knowledge accumulated by Indians in the Diaspora. It has been a pioneer in the development of ICT parks, where the needed infrastructure and social environment have been created to support the IT industry. Finally, it has actively sought to attract large multinationals through different incentive schemes.

However, India faces formidable competition in the near future from other emerging markets, and maintaining its competitive advantage will be a challenge. In order to do this, it cannot afford to stop investing in the upgrade of its ICT infrastructure to boost penetration, especially in rural areas; improve regulatory efficiency; increase IT literacy among the population; favor IT applications for the domestic economy to make production more efficient; and improve governance through e-government initiatives (Utz and Dahlman 2005).

Continuing Challenges

Despite being a pioneer in the ICT revolution, India must broaden the scope of its reforms in order to join the wider knowledge revolution. In order to do so, it will have to keep investing and avoid losing ground on the three key pillars of ICT infrastructure, education, and innovation. Infrastructure will need more investment and deeper penetration to reach a larger number of people. Education will have to be more socially inclusive. This will ensure that the Indian workforce maintains its competitive advantage over those of rivals in the knowledge revolution and that a suitably large cadre of skilled professionals is created, but it will also lift people out of poverty. Innovation will have to be encouraged at all levels, especially in production techniques, supply chain management, and logistics, rather than be restricted to frontier fields such as IT, chemicals, and engineering products.

Moreover, India cannot afford to forget about a key pillar of the knowledge economy—the business environment. Despite embarking on a broad program of market reforms since 1991, India still has some way to go to become an open market economy, as significant barriers to firm entry/exit, FDI, trade, and more efficient institutional practices exist. Without a conducive business environment, India will be deprived of the support of an overarching framework in its quest to become a knowledge economy.

Finally, India will have to focus on further strengthening the partnership it has been working to build among the government, the private sector, and civil society (Utz and Dahlman 2005). By involving these three key players, India's adoption of a holistic approach to systematically integrate the changes made in each of the knowledge economy pillars can be made easier.

What Can Nigeria Learn from India's Experience?

Nigeria can take inspiration from India and give due attention to the knowledge economy by setting up a body along the lines of India's National Knowledge Commission to chart the way forward. This would help the country identify the key issues to be tackled under the different pillars of the knowledge economy. Moreover, it could learn from India's failure to appreciate the importance of prioritizing these identified actions and sketch out a comprehensive plan to embark on the knowledge economy revolution.

India's successful experience with ICT parks can also be of inspiration. Nigeria could consider ways to establish such parks and attract multinational companies by providing the needed infrastructure and incentives and moving beyond the failed attempts of the past. Given the dire state of the power sector in Nigeria, establishing IT parks with a dedicated power supply could be a viable way to start attracting foreign know-how that otherwise would not come to set up shop in the country. In this context, the spread of IT literacy among the population, especially in future graduates, is an essential complement.

Nigeria could consider supporting well-performing academic institutions to develop them into the equivalent of India's IITs. Through a trustworthy accreditation system, the influx of funding, and the creation of partnerships between tertiary institutions and the private sector, a handful of centers of excellence could emerge and provide the highly skilled workforce that could attract foreign and domestic companies into modern business lines. This could then put in motion a virtuous circle with the diffusion of knowledge to other areas of the economy and the progressive strengthening of the whole education system.

Finally, Nigeria could follow India's example in exploiting reverse engineering techniques, while fostering a culture of respect for IPRs. Following squabbles over pharmaceutical patents, India has shown an ability to adapt to international rules on property rights, while maintaining a competitive edge in the production of cheaper generic drugs that have won it large market shares in many countries. Moreover, it has seen the intensification of agreements between top pharmaceutical corporations and local Indian firms and conglomerates, fostering knowledge diffusion.

Notes

1. For example, the India Planning Commission's *India as a Knowledge Superpower: Strategy for Transformation* and *India Vision 2020* or the High-Level Strategic Group's *India's New Opportunity, 2020.*

2. The establishment followed previous work done on *India as a Knowledge Superpower* by a task force set up by the India Planning Commission in 2001.

3. More than 100 million Indian children remain out of school, despite the introduction of the "Sarva Shiksha Abhiyan—Education for All" program in 2001. A huge gap also exists in access to secondary education, especially for girls (Kingdon 2007).

CHAPTER 7

China Opening Up to Knowledge Economy Possibilities

China's ability to maintain its current rates of growth will depend on investments in the KE. At almost 1.3 billion, China's population is estimated to be 1.6 times the size of the populations of the United States, the European Union (EU), and Japan, combined. With such a large population and despite great economic disparities, the country has been able to enjoy long periods of stellar growth (averaging 9 percent per annum for decades). For China to maintain high growth rates and raise the living standards of its population, the country will need to invest in new KE techniques and sectors that will make it more competitive.

China's astronomical growth advances have been the result of the country's ability to provide low-cost assembly-line manufacturing. By the beginning of the next decade, China could become the largest exporter in the world, accounting for an estimated 10 percent of global trade. This rapid growth in China's trade can primarily be attributed to its ability to provide cheap goods for export and progressively increase the technological content of such goods. The country has been able to successfully and efficiently provide assembly-line services for the production of ICT goods, in particular. They now account for the largest proportion of China's exports, or one-third, up from slightly more than 12 percent of total trade in 1996. In 2004, China ranked as the world's largest exporter of IT products, outstripping the EU, Japan, and the United States, with its major IT exports being computer and communications equipment (figure 7.1).

China is currently facing major challenges in its transition toward a knowledge- and services-based economy. In 2005, the country produced 303 million mobile phones and 81 million computers, taking second place as the world's largest PC maker. It also became the world's third-largest producer of semiconductors, according to the Organisation for Economic Co-operation and Development (OECD 2006). China is making a rapid transition to a services-based economy, with travel services (tourism) and communications services becoming the country's largest exports (figure 7.2). China's pace of IT manufacturing has drastically brought down IT costs globally. Although the country's advances in manufacturing have been impressive, China has only recently begun to confront the limitations of the sources of its growth, coming from low-cost manufacturing and imported and assimilated technology.

China has been opening itself up to competition with its recent accession to the World Trade Organization (WTO). China's agreement with the WTO requires that it will create a level playing field for domestic and foreign firms. The country will need to find a comparative advantage in order to remain competitive in the global economy. The conditions for economic competition in China remain poor and strongly impacted by

Figure 7.1   China: A Major ICT Export Hub

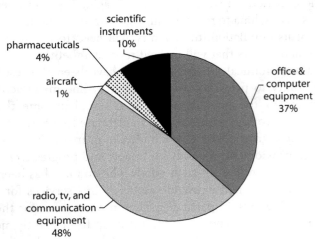

Source: OECD 2004.

Figure 7.2   China Increases Travel Services; India Increases Communications Exports

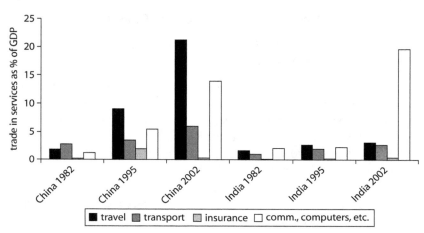

Source: OECD database.

monopolies, obscure procurement policies, protected markets, and inter-provincial barriers to trade (OECD 2004). By joining the WTO, China has agreed to undertake a series of important commitments to liberalize its regulatory framework in order to integrate into the world economy and provide a more predictable environment for trade and foreign invest-ment in accordance with WTO rules (box 7.1).

Existing tariff and nontariff barriers to internal trade diminish the potential of China's large internal market for realizing economies of scale and scope, and the removal of these barriers will allow the coun-try to take full advantage of its large market. With international com-petition increasing, it will no longer be enough to import or copy high-end technologies from the United States and Europe. If China is to find a place in the world economy, it needs to shift to producing higher-value-added goods in order to support future waves of eco-nomic growth.

As China increasingly exposes itself to intense global competition, the country is accordingly looking to foster domestic innovation to carry it through the next stage of development. China differs from its neighbors in that it has long encouraged heavy inward investment. Of the 55 percent of China's total exports that are attributed to production and assembly-related activities, 58 percent of these are driven by foreign enterprises, of which 38 percent are entirely foreign-owned. In fact, not one of the

Box 7.1

Accession to the WTO Entails Important Changes

China has committed to the World Trade Organization on a set of trade reforms that will have a far-reaching impact on its economy:

- China will provide nondiscriminatory treatment to all WTO members. All foreign individuals and enterprises, including those not invested or registered in China, will be accorded treatment no less favorable than that accorded to enterprises in China with respect to the right to trade.
- China will eliminate dual-pricing practices, as well as differences in treatment accorded to goods produced for sale in China in comparison to those produced for export.
- Price controls will not be used for purposes of affording protection to domestic industries or services providers.
- The WTO agreement will be implemented by China in an effective and uniform manner by revising its existing domestic laws and enacting new legislation fully in compliance with the WTO agreement.
- Within three years of accession, all enterprises will have the right to import and export all goods and trade them throughout the customs territory, with limited exceptions.

Source: World Bank 2007.

top 10 high-technology companies is Chinese (OECD 2006). Much of the IT assembly takes place in China, with components often imported from Japan, Taiwan (China), the United States, and Europe. In response to the country's domestic innovation weaknesses, China has enacted a series of policies to transition from being a low-cost manufacturer to being a global provider of high-value-added products, such as software, information security, and IT services. In its most recent five-year national plan, covering 2006–11, the Chinese government announced its intent to foster domestic innovation in all high-tech sectors through greater investment and domestically owned patents, and to reduce its dependence on foreign technology.

China's ability to embrace the knowledge economy has been hindered by constrained markets and low tertiary education enrollments. As it embraces free markets and increases its tertiary enrollments (particularly in the sciences), China has been reaping some of the benefits of the knowledge economy. A poor IPR regime and weak rule of law initially allowed Chinese companies to blossom by replicating pirated technologies from overseas. However, given China's current stage of development, this has become an obstacle to increased investment and the authorities are working on improving IPR and patent protection. China has large and diverse provinces that differ greatly in natural and human resource endowments and in economic performance and welfare indicators. Prosperous areas include Beijing, Shanghai, and Tianjin. Parts of the poorest provinces appear to be several centuries behind in their technology and living standards. Beijing and Shanghai, the most knowledge-intensive areas in China, have knowledge intensities 6.1 and 5.3 times the national average, respectively (OECD 2004). Given the similar diversities in regional development in Nigeria, China's experiences present several important lessons for Nigeria.

China's limited international trading links to the rest of the world until recently has resulted in a lack of competitive pressure by the global community, an environment that is not conducive to stimulating innovation and growth. Overall, China has experienced an impressive economic performance, improving human development, and exceptional growth rates. The scorecard (figure 7.3) demonstrates that China's economy is still relatively protected from international

Figure 7.3   China's Current Position in Knowledge Economy

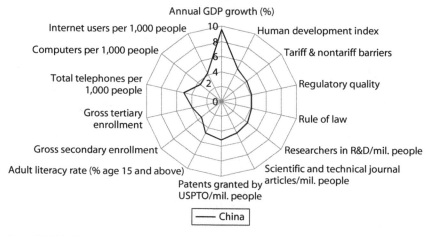

Source: World Bank Knowledge Economy Methodology Database 2009.

competition, with low scores for tariff and nontariff barriers. China is average in its use of FDI as a way of obtaining global knowledge, but it does poorly in its domestic R&D and in the technological intensity of its exports. It also scores poorly in the indicators for the rule of law and control of corruption. The country does fairly well on adult literacy, but less well on secondary enrollment rates, and even worse on tertiary enrollment rates. The absolute number of enrollments in and graduates from tertiary education in China match the numbers in the United States and the EU. Although large in absolute numbers, only a small portion of the population in China has a tertiary education degree. China's level of enrollments in and graduation from advanced research programs, such as PhDs, is also significantly lower compared to other economies, although this is changing rapidly.

Recent Issues and Continuing Challenges for China's Knowledge Economy

Economic and Institutional Regime Issues

A considerable amount of China's economic growth has been fueled by significant changes in government economic policies, which have progressively given market forces greater autonomy. China is now in the middle of a significant transformation from a command economy to a market-driven society. The momentum toward a freer economy has continued, with membership in the WTO leading to the reform of a large number of China's laws and regulations, and the prospect of further tariff reductions. In 2005, regulations that prevented privately owned companies from entering a number of sectors in the economy, such as infrastructure, public utilities, and financial services, were abolished, permitting the emergence of a powerful private sector. The government has also introduced reforms into the state-owned sector that dominated the economy in the early 1990s. Some state-owned enterprises have fairly recently been transformed into corporations and, as a result, the number of state-controlled industrial enterprises fell by more than one half in the following five years. This transformation was supported and facilitated by the introduction of more flexible employment contracts and the creation of unemployment and welfare programs (OECD 2004).

However, China's market incentives and institutions, despite considerable progress, still constrain the economy from taking full advantage of rapid advances in global knowledge. China's institutions remain legacies of the command economy and of the traditional Chinese conceptions of the state and society, which encourage the allocation of resources based on privilege and familiarity rather than viability and productivity, causing inefficiencies in business and innovation. China's legal system, in particular, has been regarded as being extraordinarily complex and unclear, due to the many uncoordinated legal initiatives of the different levels of government. Corruption, weak enforcement mechanisms, and inadequately trained and underpaid judges are all staples within China's rule of law. Tax collection in China is also underdeveloped; the tax revenue of the central and provincial governments is just 14 percent of gross national product, which is less than half the average for OECD countries. As a result, the government is forced to finance its spending through off-budget funds from banks.

China's financial system remains underdeveloped and is dominated by the banking sector, which is more than three times larger than the stock market. In the past, the bulk of lending went to state-owned enterprises (SOEs), with the rest distributed to support public policies. But many distressed SOEs started defaulting on their loans, creating a high level of nonperforming loans in the banking system. To some extent this is still the case and state-directed lending is still practiced, constraining the private sector's access to credit. This is because banks do not allocate their capital efficiently, or according to transparent lending practices and market-based rules. Thus, most of firm financing comes from retained earnings and informal sources, which limit the speed with which firms can expand and provide productive employment (Dahlman and Aubert 2001).

China's government will have to reduce its direct influence on the economy and simply guide the market to promote a knowledge-driven system. The government will need to create agencies for consumer protection; guard against anticompetitive practices; remove barriers to private development and foreign participation in services, where excessive regulation has constrained growth; strengthen the financial sector by increasing the autonomy of Chinese banks, permitting them to allocate capital more efficiently by instituting risk-based, rather than policy-based lending practices; and further develop the stock and insurance markets.

Innovation System Issues

The reform of the 1980s focused on pushing enterprises to be the driving force of science and technology (S&T) and R&D activities. Since the beginning of the reforms of China's national innovation system in the 1980s, which sought to change the country's Soviet-style R&D system, the government has implemented two large-scale national S&T programs that aim to foster high-quality fundamental research and to facilitate the commercialization of technology. In China, the ICT industry is the most dynamic sector of the economy, and there is evidence of fast improvement of domestic firms' technological capability. The rapid evolution of the ICT infrastructure (telephone mainlines, mobile phones, PCs, and the Internet) has contributed to knowledge creation, codification, and diffusion, and forged a linkage between China's knowledge network and the global knowledge network.

China's new science and technology program seeks to foster domestic innovation on all levels in a way that the reforms were unable to do. In January 2006, China's Science and Technology Congress met for three days to approve a medium- to long-term science and technology program. The program identified priorities for the next 15 years and confirmed the aim of boosting investment in science and technology to 2 percent of GDP by 2010, and 2.5 percent by 2020. In 2006, China for the first time spent more on research and development, at just over US$136 billion, than Japan, and so became the world's second-biggest investor in R&D after the United States. Reaching the targets of the S&T program will require investment in 2020 to be six times what it is today (Hepeng 2007).

The medium- to long-term plan determines 68 priority goals spread across 11 key areas of importance to China's economy and development, including energy, environment, agriculture, manufacturing, transport, and public health. The plan also seeks to embark on 16 special research projects focused on core electronic devices, extremely large-scale integrated circuit manufacturing technologies, wideband wireless mobile communications technology, breeding new transgenic biological varieties, developing a large-scale advanced pressurized water reactor, prevention of infectious diseases such as AIDS and hepatitis, R&D for giant airplanes, and manned space flights. Eight cutting-edge technology areas and four major new research programs in protein research, nanoscience, growth and reproduction, and quantum modulation research will be implemented in upcoming years.

China's Innovation Strengths

Chinese policy is becoming more outward facing, as the government starts to think in terms of an integrated national system of innovation to meet the goals of its S&T program. China has a great chance of meeting the aforementioned goals because the government maintains the ability to mobilize resources, and the country has the world's largest scientific workforce, a high output of scientific papers, and a successful strategy to attract overseas talent back to the country. Second, traditional forms of state planning and control are being replaced by a lighter touch, with enabling frameworks, including new funding structures and performance measures, and a far greater role of enterprise and private sector R&D. Third, there has been a marked improvement in the university sector, both in terms of the quantity of graduates, with around 350,000 IT graduates in 2004, and in the quality of degrees and PhDs. China now counts more researchers than Japan, and is on its way to potentially overtake the EU as well. Finally, China has stepped up the internationalization of its research system, with extensive networks of collaboration across Europe, Japan, and the United States, and a more visible presence in international journals and conferences. China's spending on R&D as a percentage of GDP, known as R&D intensity, has more than doubled from 0.6 percent of GDP in 1995 to just over 1.2 percent in 2004 (figure 7.4). In 2004, the expenditure on research and development activities for the whole country was Y184.3 billion (US$27 billion), up 19.7 percent over 2003, accounting for 1.35 percent of national GDP (OECD 2005).

Weaknesses in China's Innovation System

China needs to improve its dissemination of technology and facilitate a greater transfer of knowledge from the most efficient producers to the least efficient. Technology diffusion is fundamentally important for technological upgrading, but Chinese industries devoted very limited efforts and resources to technological diffusion in the past, preferring the import of

Figure 7.4   China Increasing R&D over Time

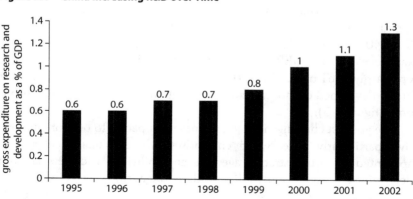

Source: OECD 2004.

technology. The absence of technology transfer channels to diffuse research results from publicly funded research institutes to industry is another major impediment to the Chinese innovation system. Furthermore, because industries, universities, and R&D institutions belong to different administrative systems in China, it prevents the free flow of resources and knowledge among them.

Market institutions are still underdeveloped and ineffectively regulated. A better-functioning market economy is a prerequisite for efficient knowledge and technology dissemination. Through joint funding to local and provincial governments, the central government should give higher priority and greater resources to technology dissemination schemes: engineering, research and productivity centers, upgraded programs for rural industries, extension services in agriculture, and regional technical centers to support small- and medium-size enterprises. Incentives are lacking for Chinese enterprises to devote their resources to R&D because returns on investment in other activities tend to be higher and more immediate. This market environment has discouraged Chinese enterprises from undertaking R&D and other efforts to improve their product qualities and technical standing (OECD 2004).

Private-Sector Participation in R&D

Chinese enterprises, particularly SOEs, do not invest sufficiently in R&D. A significant amount of China's growth and development has relied on imported technologies, demonstrated by the low 0.03 percent of Chinese firms that own the intellectual property rights of the core of the technologies they use. This acts as a serious constraint on profitability in the long run. In terms of R&D intensity and patenting, Chinese enterprises spend on average only 0.56 percent of turnover, while larger firms spend a lowly 0.71 percent. China's business R&D has increased slowly from 40 percent to 45 percent of total gross expenditures on research and development (GERD) between 1991 and 1998, after which it shot up sharply to 61 percent in 2002. The current level is not far behind that of the developed economies, and thus quite high for a developing economy (figure 7.5).

The greatest challenge is to get Chinese companies to be more innovative, particularly state-owned enterprises, where management is still appointed by administrative agencies and individuals' careers are not determined, or significantly influenced, by the performance of the enterprises they manage. Because many of these managers' posts are of a political nature, and managers are likely to be reassigned to a new post in a few

Figure 7.5   China's Private Sector Takes Lead in R&D Expenditures

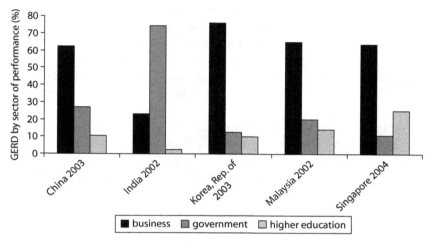

Source: UNESCO database.

Note: The fuller the scorecard, the better poised a country is to embrace the knowledge economy.

years, managers tend to be more interested in working on short-term, low-risk issues. Because investment in R&D often carries high risk and may take a long time to deliver economic returns, R&D tends to be treated as a low priority by SOE managers. Because of this low priority, management of technological innovation is weak in Chinese enterprises. Yet, under a planned economy, SOEs are connected to state development plans and are therefore in a favorable position to receive state allocations of various funds for innovation and technological upgrading. Moreover, they enjoy better access to the capital market for financing. While resources have been channeled to SOEs that lack the incentive to undertake R&D, smaller and nonstate enterprises, which are more motivated to innovate, cannot get the resources they need. Thus it is paramount that a greater percentage of finance is distributed to nonstate enterprises (OECD 2004).

Plagiarism and Misconduct

Protection policies must be strengthened in order to encourage people and enterprises to innovate and generate publications and patents. Because there are substantial benefits associated with scientific findings, a large number of people tend to plagiarize results, making research collaboration difficult. As a result, most researchers are said to work with their door closed. This practice is inefficient and bad for innovation as it blocks technology dissemination. China's shares in patent grants or applications at the U.S. Patent and Trademark Office and the European Patent Office are still very small. However, the level of international cooperation in science and technology, measured by patent applications owned or co-owned by foreign residents and patents with foreign co-inventors, is actually higher for China than for most large economies. Chinese enterprises are adversely affected by the poor protection of IPRs. Enterprises find little incentive to invest in their own R&D and innovation and instead simply rely on copying and imitating other firms' production technologies and product designs. Those that do put resources into R&D see their interests hampered by the lack of protection for their discoveries (World Bank 2005b).

Inadequate R&D Personnel

China's supply of R&D personnel is currently inadequate to meet the needs of the ambitious science and technology development program (figure 7.6). The quality of Chinese R&D personnel is generally low and unsatisfactory, and the problem stems from the Chinese education system, which emphasizes theoretical and exam-oriented learning at the expense of lifelong learning and problem-solving skills. This is further worsened by the lack of investment in personnel training in the enterprise sector, which limits the upgrading of knowledge by technical personnel. Furthermore, China has experienced a major brain drain in the past two decades, with a large number of educated Chinese going abroad to study and the majority having not yet returned to China.

Figure 7.6   China Needs More Researchers

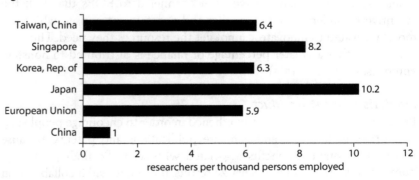

researchers per thousand persons employed

Source: OECD 2004.

Education Issues

China has been able to provide students who are not able to get into public universities with an effective alternative in privately funded tertiary institutions. In higher education, the government deserves credit for encouraging the mergers of small, single-discipline institutions to broaden the education of students and lower the unit costs. Public higher education system authorities have a very selective student recruitment program, creating intense competition for these seats. Because of the limited access to institutions of higher education, self-study for the state-administered higher education qualification examination has become an alternative. In addition to China's public higher education system, and an independent military higher education system, a large informal private higher education system has grown rapidly since the early 1980s. Privately funded tertiary institutions are nonprofit entities that derive revenues from tuition and boarding fees. They offer a limited range of professional and practical courses and attract students unable to get into public universities (OECD 2004).

However, a large number of Chinese students still prefer to go abroad in order to receive well-rounded educations. China should develop more high-quality teaching universities domestically to educate its students, reduce the need to finance education abroad, and even attract more foreign students to China. Other countries, particularly the United States, are benefiting from Chinese scholars who enroll in those countries' universities in order to receive an education that focuses on soft as well as hard skills (figure 7.7). China's higher education institutions have, instead, limited

Figure 7.7   Influx of Scholars in United States: Largest Share from China

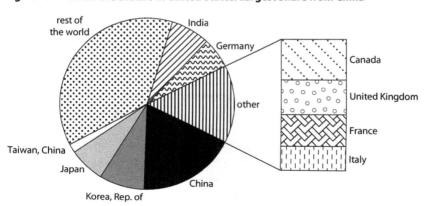

Source: OECD 2004.

autonomy in managerial, financial, and pedagogical matters. They lack choice in determining academic offerings, the number of students they can admit, and the tuition they charge.

China needs to pay more attention to soft skills to develop its private sector. The country needs to pay more attention to finance, law, accounting, design, marketing, education, technology, consulting, management, human resource development, foreign language fluency, and the ability to work in teams. Some of these softer skills have been underdeveloped because of the traditional emphasis on mastering hard skills. In order to attract back Chinese students from abroad and bring more foreign students to Chinese universities, the country will need to update its education system with a more modern curriculum that focuses on these soft skills that will be significant for the knowledge economy.

Vocational Education

China needs to limit the high enrollment rates in vocational schools until the competencies taught there are broadened and the curricula improved. Vocational schools currently make up a large part (60 percent) of China's secondary education system and the qualifications they provide are too narrow, mainly due to the numerous, overdetailed specifications from the planned economy. The vocational and training system should put more emphasis on general competencies that promote adaptability and lifelong learning, and less on job-specific skills. The economy needs skills in technology, software, management, and services. It also needs core skills that people can transfer across occupations and industries, like entrepreneurism, foreign language, social, and teamwork (World Bank 2005b). Most observers agree that China should encourage more students to go through a standard secondary education.

Updating Curriculum

Funding increases should be used for quality inputs and modernizing the curriculum. Although modern techniques are being increasingly incorporated into Chinese curricula, more emphasis needs to be placed on problem solving. Use of advanced information technologies are already leading to substantial changes in the Chinese education system. Innovative methods are being developed and used to deliver better education, e.g. in service training for primary and secondary school teachers; training in communications and agriculture through cable television, satellite television, and online training. However, the curriculum needs to focus more on problem solving and practical skills.

More resources need to go to rural areas. More than 60 percent of education spending goes to the primary and junior secondary segment. Poor areas lack resources for education investments—a gap widened by the private funding available in more affluent regions. New methods of training, new learning materials, and more well-trained teachers are needed. Public schools lack the resources and flexibility to adjust to the needs of the rapidly changing economy and society, while private schools, which possess greater resources and autonomy, have a competitive edge in developing new curricula and teaching methods (OECD 2004).

Information Infrastructure

Most of China still has limited and poor-quality access to information infrastructure, but the digital divide is decreasing. China still lags behind most East Asian countries in telephones, computers, and Internet connections per capita (figure 7.8) Telephone subscriptions are increasing at a fast rate, with mobile phone subscribers overtaking fixed-line subscribers in October 2003. Even though the absolute number of Internet subscribers is large, it is small in relation to the whole population. At the end of 2005, China had 111 million Internet users, amounting to just 8 percent of the population, compared with 50 percent in OECD countries. The number of broadband users stood at 64.3 million. In terms of Internet users, there

Figure 7.8   Low Teledensity Levels in Mainland China

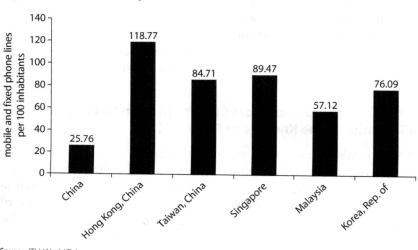

Source: ITU, World Telecommunication/ ICT Indicators 2004.

is a trend toward bridging the regional digital divide, with a decrease in the share of Internet users in the municipalities of Beijing and Shanghai, as well as the eastern coastal province of Guangdong, and an increase in the share of the western region.

While low IT costs brought by China's competitive cost structure have helped OECD-based firms reorganize and boost productivity, the actual uptake of IT within Chinese firms is lagging. Notions like supply chain management, resource planning, or knowledge management software, which are standard in OECD firms, are still undeveloped in China. Access to IT by the Chinese population is variable, with a wide digital divide between urban and rural areas (OECD 2006). China will need to decrease the digital divide within its country and find an efficient way of bringing about connectivity to a larger share of its population.

As with most telecom industries, a greater level of competition will result in a larger share of the population having access to ICT services. China will need to promote greater competition by further opening markets dominated by China Telecom and other SOEs, create an independent regulatory body, and open up to more foreign investment as a source of capital and technical expertise for information technology services. The country should promote greater use of information and communication technologies throughout the economy, such as: giving technical support to small- and medium-size enterprises; improving the efficiency of the banking system, including electronic banking, payment systems, and a national credit rating system; delivering Internet-based education and health services; and promoting electronic commerce (business to consumer and business to business) (World Bank 2001). China has made big strides, but telephone penetration, computer use, and Internet access, especially in rural and periurban areas, are still lagging and desperately need to be improved in order to create a knowledge-enabling society.

What Can Nigeria Learn from China's Efforts in Making a Transition to the Knowledge Economy?

Nigeria needs to begin fostering domestic innovation in order to remain competitive in the knowledge economy. China is beginning to recognize the need to reform its economy and promote the development of domestic innovation. However, China is facing great challenges in moving toward a more knowledge-based economy because it maintains a relatively stringent political regime. The main issue for Nigeria will be developing an innovative culture, which has proved to be a significant challenge in recent years. China is still in its early stages of making a transition to the knowledge economy, but what Nigeria can learn from China is that a history of having a closed economy is difficult to overcome, and integrating into the global community will take much more time. Because Nigeria is also in its beginning stages of knowledge development, the country should put great effort into strengthening innovation-enabling factors. At a later stage, it will need to put a stronger IPR regime and other protection policies in place. This will allow the country to innovate in an effective and efficient manner when it begins to develop a stronger and more powerful research and development base.

CHAPTER 8

The Republic of Korea: Coordination as Key to the Knowledge Economy

Korea's sustained rapid growth rate is due to its strategic use of knowledge for development. Korea has had consistent growth over the past four decades, which has enabled it to overcome the economic and social damage caused by World War II and the Korean War. Korea's past left many with the notion that it would take decades to recover and rebuild after these events. However, after 45 years, Korea's GDP per capita has increased to more than US$12,000. Korea's growth is significantly credited to its ability to use knowledge effectively in all sectors of the economy. Although Korea had not conceived an explicit knowledge economy development strategy, its commitment to strengthening each pillar through a focus on coordinating knowledge according to industry needs, led the country to rapid growth in the years following the wars (figure 8.1).

Economic, Social, and Industrial Coordination

Korea's growth has been the direct result of its ability to strategically reform various sectors in accordance with industry trends. From 1950 to the present, government prioritized achieving sustained productivity growth by consistently increasing the domestic value added of its goods (World Bank 2006).

Figure 8.1   Korea's Investment in Innovation and ICT Spurs Knowledge Economy

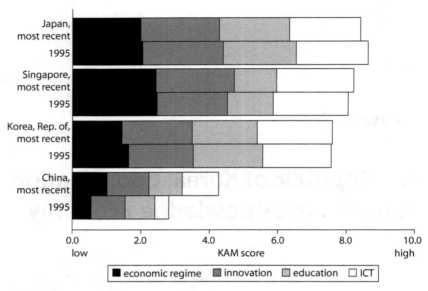

Source: World Bank Knowledge Assessment Methodology 2009.

Korea began with investments in education and the use of licensed technology. In the 1960s, Korea began investing in both export promotion and import substitution, starting with subsistence agriculture and labor-intensive light manufacturing sectors such as textiles and bicycles. In order to meet the industries' needs, considerable amounts of capital were invested in primary education. And technologies, obtained through foreign licensing, were adapted for domestic production, allowing for a gradual shift up the value-added chain toward more sophisticated products.

Moving up the value chain required investments in technical and vocational training. In the mid-1970s, Korea began the development of its heavy industries such as chemicals and shipbuilding, and policies were subsequently enacted to improve the technological capabilities of the country. This transition was further facilitated and supported by Korea's incentive to improve the access to and quality of technical and vocational training.

Deregulation and further investments in higher education continued to spur growth. In the 1980s, Korea attempted to ensure a market-conducive environment by deregulating various sectors and liberalizing trade. The government also expanded higher education while investing in indigenous research and development through the establishment of an R&D program. The country continued to pursue high-value-added manufacturing through the 1990s by promoting indigenous high-technology innovation.

Korea's early growth has been a direct result of the country's ability to coordinate government policies and investment in education and innovation with market needs (World Bank 2006). But there came a time when the government's mechanism of resource allocation, which had been effective when the economy was growing quickly, was no longer effective. When the economy became larger and more complex, this approach no longer produced stellar growth outcomes.

The Asian crisis of 1997 prodded the government to undertake widespread economic reforms. The old policy framework and institutions that had led Korea in the early high-growth era turned out to be liabilities for sustained economic growth in the new economic environment. In response, Korea began undertaking reforms in the public sector and labor markets in order to overcome the crisis and ensure rapid economic recovery. In 1998, following the crisis, Korea launched a national campaign to make the transition to an advanced knowledge-based economy in which domestic innovation would thrive. By using the framework developed by the Knowledge for Development program of the World Bank, Korea has since evolved into a mature knowledge-based economy by assigning priority to and investing in knowledge inputs, rather than physical capital (World Bank 2006c).

Reforming Korea's Market Structure through Deregulation

The Korean government, in an effort to bolster the business environment, improved the rule of law through greater transparency, disclosure of information, and increased accountability for both the public and private sectors. Since the 1997 crisis, the Korean government has relied more on market mechanisms and the private sector to take a lead in generating economic activity. Government has deregulated the economy, and promoted competition and entrepreneurship.

After the crisis, in order to rehabilitate the financial system, the government liquidated troubled institutions, wrote off nonperforming loans, and recapitalized promising financial institutions. In the corporate sector, the Korean government implemented initiatives to improve corporate governance systems, revise bankruptcy procedures, and remove anticompetitive regulations. Korea created more flexible labor markets. For example, labor laws were revised to legalize layoffs, and a legal framework for manpower-leasing services was introduced. Unemployment insurance, a well-functioning pension system, and properly targeted poverty programs were all developed as part of the state insurance package. In addition, the government promoted the formation of a venture capital market, which has grown rapidly since the late 1990s. Korea is now one of the leading countries in terms of venture capital investment as a share of GDP (World Bank 2006).

Developing a Demand-Driven Education System

Korea's education system was nurtured and expanded according to the manpower needs of the economy. In the 1950s and 1960s, education policies focused on the expansion of primary and secondary education, which was critical to supply at least a literate workforce to the soft manufacturing industries. Vocational high schools were also established and developed in the 1960s to provide training in craft skills for the growing labor-intensive light manufacturing industries. Junior vocational colleges were set up in the 1970s to supply technicians for the heavy and chemical industries.

In the 1980s, the higher education expansion policies adopted by the government were instrumental in supplying high-quality professional workers and R&D personnel that were required as Korea began developing its domestic innovation system (World Bank 2006c). Each level and entity within Korea's education system has been strengthened, demonstrated by Korea's KAM scorecard for education (figure 8.2). It shows that enrollment is extremely high at the tertiary and secondary levels, and achievements in math and science subjects are even more remarkable. Korea has also been able to supply value-added inputs to education, e.g., high levels of Internet access in schools and high-quality science and math education.

Korea's progress in creating an efficient education system is the result of significant investments by both the public and private sectors. In 2002, 7.1 percent of GDP was spent on education, a level much higher than the OECD average of 5.8 percent. The only OECD countries to surpass this figure were Iceland, the United States, and Denmark. Public financing of the education system increased more than 27-fold in real terms between 1963 and 1995, whereas Korea's GDP increased only 14-fold during the same period.

Private expenditures on education are significant, accounting for 2.9 percent of GDP, compared to the OECD average of 0.7 percent

Figure 8.2   Korean and Chinese Education

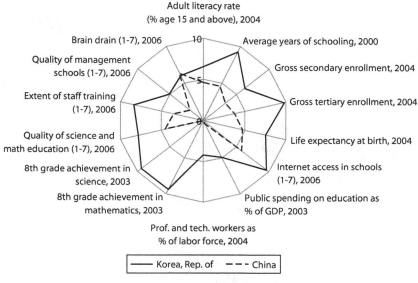

Adult literacy rate
(% age 15 and above), 2004

Brain drain (1-7), 2006

Quality of management
schools (1-7), 2006

Extent of staff training
(1-7), 2006

Quality of science and
math education (1-7), 2006

8th grade achievement in
science, 2003

8th grade achievement in
mathematics, 2003

Prof. and tech. workers as
% of labor force, 2004

Public spending on education as
% of GDP, 2003

Internet access in schools
(1-7), 2006

Life expectancy at birth, 2004

Gross tertiary enrollment, 2004

Gross secondary enrollment, 2004

Average years of schooling, 2000

——— Korea, Rep. of   – – – China

Source: World Bank Knowledge Assessment Methodology 2009.

(World Bank 2006). The Korean government has been tremendously successful at encouraging the private sector—either households or private foundations—to bear a significant portion of total education costs (figure 8.3). Korea's culture also plays a large role in this funding as Koreans generally value education highly, and are often willing to pay more to educate their children privately. Private foundations have established a number of secondary schools and higher education institutions, in which expenses are paid by user fees. At the secondary level, enrollment at private institutions accounts for more than 40 percent of total secondary enrollment, whereas private enrollment for tertiary education exceeds 70 percent. Primary education in Korea has been treated as a public good and has been mostly publicly funded, with 99 percent of primary school students in 2005 enrolled in public schools (World Bank 2006). By encouraging the private sector to bear a significant portion of total education expenditure at the secondary and tertiary levels, government resources have been spent on key priority areas, such as offering universal primary education.

Figure 8.3   Korea's Leadership through Education

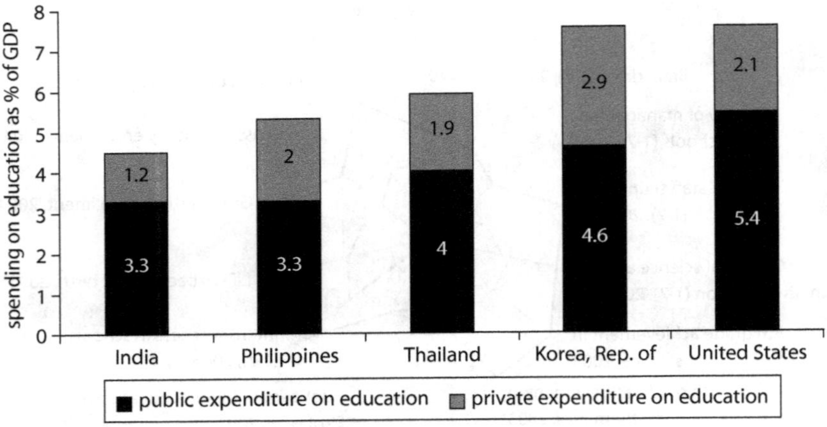

Source: UNESCO database 2009.

Developing Korea's Science and Technology Sector

Korea has developed its R&D sector by increasing the total amount of investment while simultaneously reducing government involvement. In the early post-war period, private sector R&D spending was insignificant. But growth of the innovation system required corresponding investments in technology development. Government encouraged private investment in R&D, resulting in substantial increases in R&D spending by private firms over the past four decades (figure 8.4). Consequently, the government's share of GERD has been gradually reduced and currently accounts for less than a quarter of the total. Korea's GERD has grown both in size and as a share of GDP, increasing from 0.25 percent in 1963 to 2.48 percent in 2004, according to UNESCO. These increases in R&D investment have led to corresponding increases in indigenous innovation and adoption of foreign technologies, making the country's innovation system on a par with many high-income countries.

Korea's ability to absorb, improve upon, and adapt foreign technologies to domestic production has allowed Korean industries to become internationally competitive. In the 1960s, when Korea launched its industrialization drive, it had to rely almost completely on imported foreign technologies. While doing so, the country promoted inward transfer of these foreign technologies and developed the domestic innovation and production capacity to digest, assimilate, and improve upon

Figure 8.4   Significant Increases in R&D Investment by Korea's Private Sector over Time

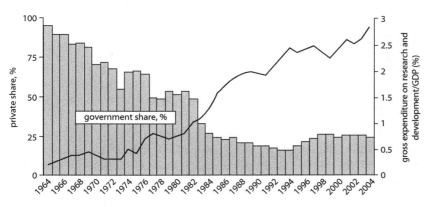

Source: World Bank Knowledge Assessment Methodology 2009.

the transferred technologies and to adapt them to domestic production. This integration process allowed Korea to reduce its dependence on FDI and avoid control by multinational corporations. By the 1980s, Korean industries had increasingly become potential competitors in the international market, making foreign companies reluctant to transfer technologies to Korea. As a result, Korea had to develop indigenous research and innovation. It did so by investing heavily in domestic R&D. This transition required highly trained scientists and engineers, as well as the financial resources necessary to support such R&D activities.

Korea's government research institutes helped meet the demand for large-scale and sophisticated R&D. In the 1960s, the Korean government borrowed heavily on international capital markets. The money was allocated to selected industries to enable firms to import capital goods, build turnkey plants, and obtain the latest technology and foreign experts needed for its technological assimilation strategy. In the 1970s, when the economy was moving into heavy industries, the government created government research institutes (GRIs) in the fields of heavy machinery and chemicals to compensate for the technological weaknesses of domestic industries. The GRIs worked with companies to enhance technological capabilities for further industrial development. The government's outward-looking, export-driven development strategy forced domestic industries into international markets, exposing them to intense global competition. To stay competitive, firms within these industries had to keep pace with technological changes by investing heavily in R&D (World Bank 2006c).

Building Information Infrastructure

Korea's excellent ICT infrastructure has been developed by a competitive private-sector telecom industry. In the early 1970s, Korea's information infrastructure was inadequate. To improve its efficiency, the Korean government focused in the 1980s and 1990s on introducing competition into the ICT sector by deregulating and liberalizing the sector and privatizing the government-owned telecom operators. From 1995 to 2003, the proportion of Koreans with cell phones increased to 70 percent, while the proportion of Internet users increased to 60 percent. Korea is now among the leading countries in the world in terms of the proportion of broadband Internet subscribers, largely due to its successful construction of ICT networks connecting all areas of the country (figure 8.5).

Excellent ICT infrastructure leads to increased uptake in e-commerce and e-government services. The number of subscribers to Internet banking services reached 22.58 million (almost 50 percent of the total population) as of March 2005, and e-commerce has increased from 50 billion won (US$43 million) in 1998 to 314 billion won (US$ 270 million) in 2004.

Figure 8.5   Korea Wired for Future

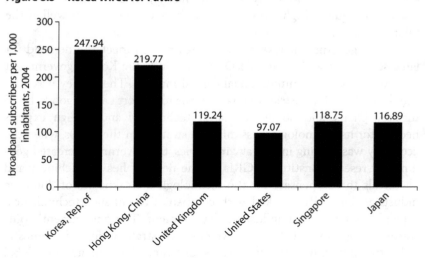

Source: International Telecommunications Union 2004.

Led by an e-government initiative, the public sector is extensively using ICT. By 2004, 97 percent of documents were dealt with through the e-approval system in the government agencies (World Bank 2006c).

Establishing a dedicated fund on a PPP basis was key to the rapid roll-out of ICT infrastructure. In order to finance the investment for the rapid deployment and overcome short-term budgetary constraints, the Informatization Promotion Fund was established. From 1993 to 2002, the fund reached a total of US$7.78 billion, 40 percent of which was from government budgetary contributions and 46 percent from private enter-prises. The funds were allocated as follows—ICT activities: 38 percent for technology development programs, 18 percent for human resources development, and the remaining 44 percent for the building of infrastruc-ture and diffusion, including standardization. Korea strategically used this fund to both narrow the digital divide and provide citizens with more dependable telecommunication services.

Continuing Challenges

Despite its achievements, Korea's education system continues to face challenges in maintaining its competitive edge. The Korean education sys-tem has yet to evolve to meet the new skill and knowledge requirements of the knowledge economy. Teacher-centered, one-way teaching, rote memorization, the lack of diversity of educational programs, and a preoc-cupation with preparing for exams have all left little room to nurture cre-ativity and initiative. Korea needs a more flexible education system that is less academic and that puts an end to tight government control over the curriculum, testing, tuition fees, and number of students in each disci-pline. These restrictions have eroded the links between educational out-put and labor-market demand. There are current mismatches in supply and demand of human resources, including shortages of highly skilled labor in strategic areas, labor shortages in small and medium enterprises, and a high degree of youth unemployment.

Critical thinking and problem solving will be the bywords of educa-tion in the future. It is increasingly important to improve students' com-petencies in critical thinking and problem solving, and to promote lifelong learning through a broader interdisciplinary approach. These objectives will only be accomplished by granting greater autonomy to the universities and giving them discretionary powers in hiring teaching staff, managing academic affairs, and setting student admission quotas (World Bank 2006). In terms of innovation, Korea is a big spender on

R&D, with most of it from the private sector, but outputs could be improved further. There will be an increasing need to update the role of GRIs; improve interaction among universities, government research institutes, and private firms; and improve the efficiency of private R&D output (Aubert 2006).

What Can Nigeria Learn from Korea's Experience?

Nigeria should strive to formulate a strategy for development that is centered on coordination with and involvement of the private sector. Korea's most significant development attribute was its ability to develop its skill and innovation base according to the needs of industry. Government played a major role in effectively making a transition from being a regulator to being an architect of the economy, making strategic decisions on guiding the country toward strengthening different sectors at various times in the country's development, and by taking a less direct interventionist approach.

Nigeria, which is beginning a transition toward becoming a major services industry hub, should begin investing in knowledge inputs that strengthen all relevant sectors of the economy. In terms of innovation, Korea invested heavily in R&D, but only after it had built up the knowledge capacity and technical base that it received from years of assimilation and imitation of technologies inherited from the global community.

Nigeria should begin investing in developing a research base geared to the process of imitation and assimilation. This will help increase the value-added of exports and begin the process of domestic innovation. Research as a discipline should be given greater funding within universities and R&D institutes, as they form the backbone of a research base.

Nigeria should support the private sector's involvement in the education sector, particularly in funding education. This would encourage competition among providers and supply the government with excess funding to be distributed toward higher education, which will be increasingly important in creating skilled workers for the emerging services industry. In the education system, Korea encouraged the private sector to finance a large portion of education expenditure, especially at the higher levels, thereby augmenting scarce public resources.

Nigeria must fast-track investments in ICT infrastructure. As Nigeria attempts to position itself as a major destination for offshoring activities, it will be even more important to have an adequate ICT infrastructure and good human resources. It is important that the country possess the skills necessary to supply the BPO sector. Nigeria can also consider establishing something along the lines of Korea's Informatization Promotion Fund. Such a fund could build upon current achievements and help to develop IT connectivity, science culture, and literacy levels within Nigeria, thereby lessening the digital divide.

CHAPTER 9

Singapore's Transition to the Knowledge Economy: From Efficiency to Innovation

Singapore's commitment to efficiency has attracted FDI that has allowed it to grow rapidly. Singapore's government has always been committed to the concept of efficiency, recognizing early on that, to compensate for the country's natural "comparative disadvantage" associated with being a small economy with a limited domestic market and population size, Singapore would need to develop a highly efficient and productive infrastructure system to help reduce production costs and attract foreign investors. This commitment to efficiency, along with the government's adoption of proactive growth strategies and a highly educated, English-speaking workforce, have made Singapore a choice production base for multinational corporations. There are currently more than 5,000 foreign companies located in Singapore and many more multinational corporations and foreign financial institutions that have established operating and manufacturing bases on the island.

Singapore has also been successful in attracting talented foreign nationals. Approximately 19 percent of Singapore's population is made up of foreign nationals. As a result of this ability to attract foreign capital and skilled foreign workers, the Singaporean economy has grown at 8.5 percent per annum in recent years, and per capita income has grown at 6.6 percent per year, roughly doubling every decade. Over the years, the economy has gradually moved into more technology-related fields. Labor-intensive industries such as textiles, once important to the island's economy, are no longer part of Singapore's economic landscape.

Like other Asian countries, Singapore reevaluated its growth strategies after the 1997 crisis. Singapore has since recognized that efficiency alone will no longer guarantee sustained growth in the future and that it will need to formulate alternative strategies for growth.

Where Does Singapore Currently Stand in the Knowledge Economy?

Singapore is good at incorporating existing technology, but lags far behind other developed countries in the ability to create new technologies. In the *Global Competitiveness Report*, Singapore was ranked 25th in terms of firm-level innovation in 2002, below most developed economies. The country ranked in the top 10 in the world in terms of technology-using indicators such as quality of school science and technology education, licensing of foreign technologies, etc. But it was rated much lower in technology-creating indicators like R&D spending, R&D personnel, availability of venture capital, and intellectual property protection.

Singapore's education system is also proving a brake on improving the KE. Singapore performs poorly in terms of entrepreneurial activities, ranking 21st among the 31 countries surveyed in the *Global Entrepreneurship Monitor Report 2003* studies (Tan 2005). Singapore's knowledge economy scorecard further emphasizes the country's weaknesses. Adult literacy levels are much lower than those of Korea and equivalent to those of China (figure 9.1). However, the scorecard also demonstrates the country's powerful economic and institutional regime, scoring remarkably high in rule of law, regulatory quality, and tariff and nontariff barriers.

Despite housing developed and active technological industries, Singapore has only recently begun to innovate domestically. Manufacturing contributes 22 percent to Singapore's GDP, with electronics accounting for half of the country's manufacturing output, while finance and business services are responsible for more than one-quarter. Manufacturing and services are the twin engines of the country's economic growth. Singapore has become the disk drive capital of the world and is home to a semiconductor hub, currently producing one-third of the world's disk drives and housing 15 chip fabrication plants. It has a 70 percent market share in the manufacture of offshore oil rigs. In aerospace, Singapore has the second-largest cluster of aerospace maintenance, repair, and overhaul activities in the world. In

Figure 9.1   Singapore's Standing on Global KE Indicators

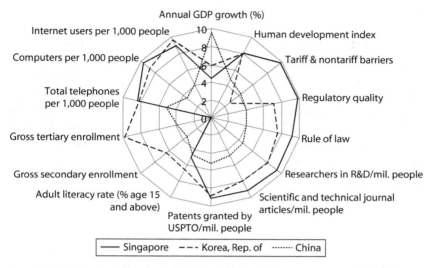

Source: World Bank Knowledge Assessment Methodology Database 2009.

biomedical sciences, six out of 10 top pharmaceutical companies manufacture in Singapore (Hwa 2003). The country has over time begun to recognize that in order to remain internationally competitive, it will have to focus on domestic innovation.

Embarking on a New Innovation Strategy

Key to Singapore's future growth is its investment in innovation over efficiency. In 2002, a high-level Economic Review Committee was organized by the government to assist the country in formulating a new development strategy. The Economic Review Committee's strategy focused on enhancing the economy's innovative capacity, with the aim of making Singapore an innovation hub for Asia. The government has since devoted more resources for R&D and innovation.

Previous five-year plans implemented by the National Science and Technology Board, starting from the early 1990s, sought to target mainly short-term applied technological innovations, with few attempts to deepen the culture and practice of innovation across the whole economy. Singapore's new innovation strategy, however, seeks to accomplish these goals by developing basic innovation and cultivating a scientific culture.

At the 2002 knowledge economy conference in Sydney, Australia, Ko Kheng Hwa, managing director of the Singapore Economic Development Board (EDB), discussed the country's strategy in making the transition to the knowledge economy without abandoning its powerful presence in manufacturing (box 9.1). He emphasized that Singapore is looking to reform its innovation system to focus on "the broad and the basic": from drug discovery to clinical development, clinical trials, process development, manufacturing, and the provision of health care services. It aims not only to promote innovations in manufacturing, services, and creative content, but to do so at firms of different sizes, from giant multinational corporations to local SMEs. To pursue these strategies, the government has

---

Box 9.1

Singapore's Strategy for Future Development

Strategy 1: Build bridges through a web of free trade agreements. These free trade area agreements, both multilateral and bilateral, will be a crucial part of Singapore's strategy to build bridges to key economies of the world, and to increase market accessibility of companies based in Singapore.

Strategy 2: Broaden the industry base and develop new growth clusters. The country will focus on new industry clusters such as biomedical and nanotechnology manufacturing, as well as on a portfolio of internationally salable services with high growth potential, such as educational services, professional services, and intellectual property management.

Strategy 3: Whether in services or manufacturing, the country will build new capabilities to move up the value chain in three particular areas. The first will be increasing the value-added of production activities, for example, into highly automated manufacturing. The second is moving upstream into R&D, innovation, and tax incentives for new ideas. The third is moving downstream into regional electronics supply chain management, market development, brand management, and intellectual property management in the Asia-Pacific region, and enlarging regional headquarters operations.

Strategy 4: Create a vibrant enterprise ecosystem by developing the venture capital industry, increasing tax incentives for new ideas, and making provisions for new users to try out the country's new inventions.

Source: Hwa 2003.

allocated US$7 billion over a five-year period to support public sector R&D, which will in turn stimulate private sector R&D (Hwa 2003).

The new plan intends to shift the focus of innovation to developing technology within small firms in the service sector. More resources are being devoted toward long-term, basic research. There is also an increased awareness that a significant part of innovation actually comes from small firms. Tapping into the innovative energy within the service sector has become a high priority. In addition to traditional service industries that thrive in Singapore, such as financial, tourism, entrepot trade, health care, transport, and logistics, the government is actively promoting the country as a regional hub in other service industries like education, legal services, and creative industries.

In order to make these transitions, the Singaporean government is investing heavily in innovation infrastructure, rather than efficiency infrastructure, deemed necessary to building up a critical mass of innovative people and innovative activities, with the immediate objective of attracting the right type of workers rather than the right type of firms (box 9.2).

Box 9.2

Crafting an Innovation Culture and the "One North" Project

In order to attract and retain creative talent, Singapore has been heavily investing in cultivating an environment that is both supportive and conducive to innovation and enterprise. Launched in December 2001, "One North" is quickly becoming a world-class R&D hub for scientists and entrepreneurs working in biomedical sciences, ICT, and media. The project is expected to be completed within 15 to 20 years of its launch. Phase I of the project has witnessed the construction of two centers of activities; Biopolis, which will serve as the focal point for biomedical sciences R&D, and Fusionpolis, which will house collections of firms involved in R&D and production work for ICT and media industries. The project will focus on the whole range of production activities, including a large portion of basic research, while promising a "total living and working environment," with not only research institutes and business offices, but also residential properties, shopping, public parks, and other facilities. It will be equipped with state-of-the-art facilities in computing network, sewage disposal, and energy-generating systems, and an internal shuttle train system.

(continued)

Box 9.2 *(Continued)*

The project claims to offer opportunities for "seamless interaction" among research scientists, entrepreneurs, and other business and services sector operators within an "enclave" environment. The project's proximity to other major tertiary institutions (e.g., the National University of Singapore, INSEAD Asia campus) makes for easy collaboration with researchers from the outside. The tenants of One North comprise both public and private research institutions and business enterprises, including the Genome Institute of Singapore and the Bioinformatics Institute. Private companies such as GlaxoSmithKline and Novartis Institute for Tropical Diseases are already set up, and Vanda Pharmaceuticals and Paradigm Therapeutics have also signed up. Many of these firms intend to undertake a wide range of activities in Singapore, from basic research and development to product and process development, clinical research, manufacturing, business headquarters, and health care delivery operations.

When fully occupied, the seven buildings in the Biopolis project will house about 4,000 researchers. Many of the researchers working in One North will likely be foreigners. To overcome the shortage of scientists in Singapore, the government is actively recruiting from abroad. Already, some acclaimed researchers have moved into the Biopolis, including Dr. Alan Colman, who cloned Dolly the sheep, and who moved from Scotland to Singapore to continue his research. Dr. Edison Liu, director of the National Cancer Institute of the United States, is now in Singapore heading the country's Genome Institute. Professor Yoshiaki Ito, one of the chief authorities on stomach cancer research in Japan, together with his team of 10, has uprooted and moved to Singapore to continue the research.

Source: Tan 2005.

There are also efforts to change the "mindset" of Singaporeans to bring out the enterprising and adventurous spirit in them, by increasing the availability of innovation-enabling infrastructure such as R&D facilities, well-defined intellectual property laws, and venture capital (Tan 2005).

IPRs and Patents

The Singaporean government is committed to protecting innovators. The government upgraded the Registry of Trade Marks and Patents to a statutory board called the Intellectual Property Office of Singapore (IPOS) in 2001 in order to formulate and regulate an entire range of intellectual property legislation. IPOS has the mandate of building an environment that promotes greater intellectual property creation, protection, and exploitation in Singapore, and has been active in developing regional and global networks, including signing various bilateral and regional treaties (with the United States, the EU, and Japan), to help extend the reach of Singapore's intellectual property community. In January 2003, IPOS also helped launch the Intellectual Property Academy, which has been mandated to help strengthen the intellectual property competency in Singapore through research and education (Tan 2005).

Venture Capital

Government support has been a key feature of the venture capital industry development since the mid-1980s. The government was instrumental in setting up early venture capital funds such as Vertex Management and EDB Ventures. In the late 1990s, it launched a US$1 billion "Technopreneurship" Investment Fund to entice leading venture capitalists in the world to use Singapore as the regional hub and to spur training for a core of venture capital professionals. Currently more than 100 venture capital firms are in Singapore, and they manage a total venture capital fund size of US$14 billion, investing in enterprises in Singapore and the region (Tan 2005). However, these venture capital funds were reluctant to finance early seed stage projects. Thus, Singapore started a unique program whereby the EDB matches dollar for dollar any third-party investor who puts money into seed stage start-ups, up to a maximum of $300,000 (Hwa 2003). This is a good example of the enterprise ecosystem that Singapore is committed to establishing.

Recent Issues and Challenges Facing Singapore's Knowledge Economy

Innovation System

In innovation, as opposed to technology assimilation, Singapore will need to take bigger risks. The Singapore government plays a very active role in innovation, both in funding as well as in setting the strategic direction of which specific industries to promote. In the early years, Singapore catered to the known requirements of multinational corporations, exploiting the shift in production bases over the course of the product cycle. It used existing technology without having to "push the frontiers." Innovation businesses, on the other hand, require a considerable amount of frontier pushing and entail a great deal of uncertainty in terms of the ingredients needed to create the necessary and sufficient preconditions for success (Tan 2005).

Singapore can develop itself into a regional hub for a number of service industries by maintaining a lighter regulatory approach. Like the manufacturing sector and innovation businesses, the service sector could leverage Singapore's strength in efficiency infrastructure. Indeed, combined with the existing hub structure in certain service industries, such strength could also give Singapore a "first-mover advantage" when making inroads into other service industries such as education, legal services, and creative industries. Given the state of development in the service sector in the region, and the fast-changing technology that makes services increasingly tradable, Singapore could still extract considerable value by merely moving closer to the global efficiency frontiers in the service sector without necessarily engaging in "frontier-pushing" innovations. More than the manufacturing sector, the growth of the services sector is influenced by changes in the regulatory policy. A lighter regulatory approach could make a big difference. The health care industry is one example. In recent years, the growth of Singapore as a regional medical hub has been hampered by a doctor shortage and restrictions on the registration of foreign doctors. This has resulted in high private medical costs and an opportunity for some other cities in the region including Bangkok, Thailand, and Malacca, Malaysia, to vie for a slice of the pie (Tan 2005).

The country's entrepreneurial base needs to be enhanced. The number of individuals involved in R&D work has increased significantly over the past few years, in large part because of the inflows of foreign researchers. But how this will translate to greater output remains to be seen. Since 2001, there was a significant increase in the number of patents filed in Singapore (figure 9.2). However, most of the patents were filed by non-Singapore residents (7,340 out of 7,580 in 2002). In Taiwan, in contrast, domestic residents filed 24,846 patents in 2002, compared with 20,196 filed by foreigners. The trend is similar for trademark registration. Singapore's ranking in the *Global Entrepreneur Monitor Report 2003* actually fell in 2003. It was ranked 15th in a group of 22 OECD/East Asian countries, compared with 11th a year earlier. In order to reverse these trends, Singapore's needs to develop entrepreneurs who are keen on commercializing their findings.

It is difficult to determine how Singapore should best focus its innovation efforts, and on which industries it should focus due to the country's market structure. It would be advantageous to focus on innovation in the high-tech manufacturing sector, an area in which Singapore has already built up a certain capacity for innovation. To capitalize on the increasing returns and agglomeration effects in innovation activities, greater resource

Figure 9.2   Singapore Increasing Innovation Record

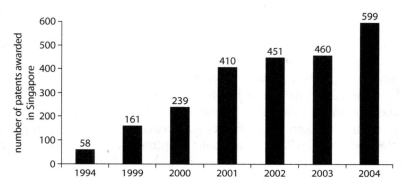

Source: World Bank Knowledge Assessment Methodology Database 2009.

specialization is often necessary. However, investment in any particular industry must be sizable enough for increasing returns to kick in. A diffused approach may not be as effective as a targeted approach. Nevertheless, concentration of resources in a few industries, in accordance with the economy's perceived comparative advantage, may require much more winner-picking and entail more risks than is comfortable for the government. "Overspecialization" in production could result in growth patterns that may be too volatile for a small city-state. Already, overreliance on the electronics industry has led to much wilder swings in GDP growth in Singapore in recent years. In this context, Singapore faces more constraints than its potential rivals in the region, such as Hong Kong (China), Seoul, and Shanghai, in terms of the strategy it can pursue and the risks it can take (Tan 2005).

The government should encourage the private sector to bear the bulk of innovation projects. The government will need to be willing to spread its resources over a wide range of industries, with the understanding that only a certain fraction of the investments will bear fruit. The government could mitigate the risk it faces by encouraging as much private-sector participation as possible and by monitoring the performance of its investments closely and frequently.

Public Sector Issues

The Singaporean government needs to loosen its regulatory grip on the economy in order to foster a more risk-taking, entrepreneurial attitude in the population. Too many rules and too harsh a stigma for nonconformist behaviors are said to have hindered Singaporeans' ability to innovate or to think independently. The society's intolerance for failure is also seen as a further hindrance to entrepreneurship. As part of the effort to encourage innovation, some attempts have been made in recent years to relax the regulatory environment and government control over the social and political lives of the population. Committees were set up to identify areas where the government may be able to loosen rules and regulations to make it easier for individuals to start and operate businesses. Schools are revamping their curricula to inculcate a stronger entrepreneurial mindset in the students (Tan 2005). Changing the culture and mindset of the population to one that is more entrepreneurial will allow Singaporeans to take bigger risks in education, innovation, and business practices.

Education Issues
Tertiary education has been assigned a high priority in recent years in order to develop the human skills necessary to facilitate the country's emerging R&D efforts. Education in Singapore is highly subsidized and constitutes the second-largest government expenditure item. The country has transformed its education system into one that is industrially targeted, able to provide the higher technical skills and worker training needed for high-technology production. In the process, the government has exercised control over curriculum content and quality, and ensured its relevance to the activities being produced. Manpower planning is effected through detailed quotas on the number of students to be admitted to specific programs (law, medicine, architecture, civil engineering, computer engineering, etc.) at tertiary institutions.

In July 2001, the country announced an incentive of about US$285 million in financial support to talented undergraduate science scholars to help fund their educations through the doctoral level. This is designed to ensure a steady supply of local research scientists to fuel growth in engineering and the sciences. In 2004, the government announced plans to devolve greater operational and financial autonomy to universities and put in place a quality assurance framework for universities to track quality enhancement. Apart from formal education, the government also directed considerable effort toward developing an industrial training system, now considered one of the best in the world for high-technology production. In addition, a new agency, the Singapore Workforce Development Agency, was established in 2003 with the specific purpose of enhancing workforce skills through developing a comprehensive, market-driven, and performance-based adult continuing education and training framework (Tan 2005).

The government is heavily encouraging research within universities through a variety of mechanisms. Funding for research programs and graduate studies has risen substantially, especially in selected areas such as life sciences, information technology, communications, and management studies. There is also aggressive recruitment of research faculty from abroad and greater research collaboration with reputable universities outside Singapore. The government, in an effort to transform the country into a regional education hub, is allocating a large amount of resources to the R&D efforts in the tertiary educational sector to enhance its research and innovation capacity.

Government grants have helped attract foreign universities to establish in Singapore. Government grants were given to set up joint research centers between local and reputable foreign universities to fund collaborative projects between them. Nine world-class universities, including the Massachusetts Institute of Technology, the Wharton School of the University of Pennsylvania, Johns Hopkins University, the University of Chicago Graduate School of Business, all from the United States; Shanghai Jiao tong University from China; and INSEAD, from France; have set up their Asian campuses in Singapore (Hwa 2003). More resources are also channeled to specific areas of study seen to be closely linked to the government's blueprint of an innovation-based economy, such as life sciences, entrepreneurial studies, and communications.

A key element of this drive for research excellence is the attraction of top researchers from abroad. Rules and regulations regarding granting of licenses for private educational institutions, programs that can be offered, and intake of foreign students have been rapidly liberalized. This is aimed at building up a critical mass of educational service providers to cater to the rising demand in the region for quality education at all levels, from secondary school to tertiary and postgraduate levels (Tan 2005).

Information Infrastructure

Singapore's commitment to liberalization and competition in information infrastructure has managed to connect a large percentage of the population. The government has implemented policies to develop an information communications sector and has aspirations for Singapore to be the information hub for the region. The state-owned monopoly, Singapore Telecoms, was partially privatized through its listing on the stock exchange in 1993 to help realize greater efficiency. Market liberalization and a pro-competition framework were established, with regulatory functions performed by the Infocomm Development Authority.

Competition has lowered prices and spurred demand in the telecom sector. As of September 2003, the mobile phone penetration rate in Singapore had reached 82 percent, the highest in Asia (figure 9.3). The Singapore ONE project, launched by the government in 1998, provides broadband infrastructure of high-capacity networks and switches, with the goal of making broadband access available to 99 percent of the population. Between 2000 and 2002, the household and corporate broadband penetration rates grew from 8 percent to 24 percent and from 15 percent to 41 percent, respectively. By June 2003, the household broadband penetration rate had increased to 31 percent, in step with the Infocomm Development Authority's target of 50 percent by 2006. The 2008 rate stood at 58.6 percent and was climbing (Tan 2005).

E-Learning and E-Government Services

Singapore has been effective in incorporating IT into schools through a uniform teacher training system offered by the Ministry of Education. The National Institute of Education is the sole teacher training institution in Singapore responsible for producing teachers effective in preparing students for knowledge for development. The programs are conducted at the diploma, degree, masters, and PhD levels. The Ministry of Education launched the IT master plan for education in April 1997 to effectively infuse ICT into education. This was a five-year, US$2 billion plan that aimed to set out a blueprint for the use of IT in schools, and to provide access to an IT-enriched school environment for every child.

Figure 9.3   Telecom Liberalization Results in Mass Access

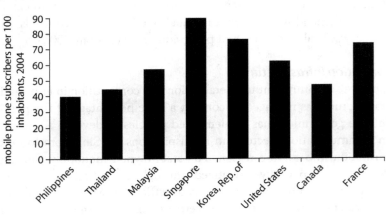

Source: International Telecommunication Union 2004.

At each phase of the implementation, primary schools were provided with an initial student-computer ratio of 6.6:1, and spent about 10 percent of their curriculum time on IT-based learning. Secondary and junior colleges started with a 5:1 student-computer ratio and devoted 10 percent of their curriculum time to IT-based learning.

The master plan provides for the eventual targets of a student-computer ratio of 2:1 and 30 percent IT-based learning curriculum time. To facilitate the move toward an ICT-enriched environment, the National Institute of Education has adopted Blackboard technology as its entry-level course delivery system, which provides the basis upon which the various e-learning models used by the National Institute of Education can be built. The templates provide an easy entry to online course development for staff members using online teaching for the first time (Cheah 2002). The program has been effective in preparing teachers in incorporating IT learning into their curricula and thus producing an IT-literate population.

The Singapore government was also one of the first in the world to implement an e-government system. The GeBIZ portal on the e-government site was the world's first Internet-based government procurement system. At the e-Citizen center, Singaporeans can obtain information and bid for certificates to register a vehicle; file their taxes; download forms to file for bankruptcy; register a marriage, baby, car, or pet; apply for a passport, housing or utilities; check their provident fund accounts or their child's school registration status; etc. (Cheah 2002).

What Can Nigeria Learn from Singapore's Innovation Strategy?

Nigeria should strengthen its R&D system and cultivate innovation in its universities. Singapore recognized early on that it needed to develop a powerful innovation sector in order to remain competitive in the knowledge economy. The country moved quickly to address the KE pillars and brought in international experience and funding wherever possible. Nigeria could adopt some of these strategies by encouraging a culture of innovation and more stringent protection of property rights. The country should also invest more heavily in university and private-sector R&D. At the moment, the country's education system deters innovation. Students are generally not encouraged to conduct or promote research or to be inquisitive.

Singapore has been able to combat a demotivating research environment by investing in attracting the right type of people through projects like One North (box 9.2), which enhance research communities. Despite the challenges that come with its international reputation, Nigeria could devote more effort to creating stronger research communities on a smaller scale, encouraging researchers to interact more intensively with one another and with peers abroad, and encourage prospects for innovation and commercialization by building links with the private sector.

Annex: Innovation—The Key to Business Growth: The Irish Story

Despite the troubled times Ireland is going through in the aftermath of the global financial crisis, the country remains a model of innovation and its story can inspire nations as they think of their prospects as knowledge-driven economies.

Collaboration and cooperation through innovation networks
Corporations today are pursuing a globally distributed, network approach to innovation. Current university programs and company R&D activities reach across borders in search of collaborative partnerships. Companies can most easily reap the rewards of innovation through a global ecosystem in which firms, universities, and governments work together.

Ireland's innovation landscape
Ireland's innovation landscape thrives on the importance of human connections. Irish business policy brings together—in a unique, no-nonsense, and highly pragmatic way—a wide range of national institutions to help create leading-edge research programs. Government, funding agencies, regulatory authorities, academia, and industry work as a team, creating a fast-growing, dynamic research environment. The result of this high-level connectivity is that Ireland has become one of the new global centers for science and innovation-based R&D. It is empowering some of the world's biggest companies to research, develop, and commercialize world-class products, processes, and services.

Long-established partnerships with global corporations have been at the core of Ireland's success in attracting leading-edge R&D activities. Despite Ireland's small size geographically, its energetic, knowledge-based economy makes it a favorite location for companies to set up their European R&D centers. In 2006, Ireland's inward investment agency, IDA Ireland, supported 54 R&D investment projects. The past year has seen R&D announcements by many prominent global

(continued)

Annex *(Continued)*

corporations. The names speak for themselves: Cisco Systems, GlaxoSmithKline, PepsiCo, Intel, IBM, Bristol-Myers Squibb. These corporations are actively supported by renowned global research organizations located in Ireland, such as the Georgia Tech Research Institute and Bell Labs.

An integrated, collaborative strategy

The Irish government pursues a carefully planned, integrated R&D strategy encompassing all of the key elements necessary to achieve world-class R&D. Its US$5 billion Strategy for Science, Technology, and Innovation will double the number of PhD graduates and attract future generations of well-educated young people into research careers in knowledge-driven companies. It will substantially extend the physical infrastructure to support them and, for the first time ever, eight government departments will coordinate all activity in relation to science, technology, and innovation.

IDA Ireland is one of the main players behind the new wave of national, collaborative R&D activity. It works closely with Science Foundation Ireland, the agency that consolidates links between industrial and academic research and funds such research. IDA Ireland and Science Foundation Ireland have developed a range of new initiatives to encourage pooled projects and attract world-class scientists to carry out research in Ireland. This bringing together of industry and academia has led to a boom in research projects. More than 10,000 researchers are working on cutting-edge R&D projects in Ireland. Many of them have relocated from the United States, Canada, Japan, the United Kingdom, Switzerland, and Belgium. Ireland's Centers for Science, Engineering and Technology link scientists and engineers in partnerships across academia and industry. One such example is the Centre for Research on Adaptive Nanostructures and Nanodevices. Its mission is to advance the frontiers of nanoscience. It provides the physical and intellectual environment for world-class fundamental research, and has partners in Irish and overseas universities.

Tax and intellectual property

Ireland's intellectual property laws provide companies with generous incentives to innovate. The Irish tax system offers huge support to turn brilliant ideas into a finished product. A highly competitive corporate tax rate of 12.5 percent is a major incentive. No tax is paid on earnings from intellectual property where the underlying R&D work was carried out in Ireland. Ireland recently introduced a new R&D tax credit designed to encourage companies to undertake new or additional

(continued)

Annex *(Continued)*

R&D activity in Ireland. It covers wages, related overhead, plant/machinery, and buildings. Stamp duty on intellectual property rights has been abolished.

People skills

The *IMD World Competitiveness Yearbook 2006* rates Ireland's education system as one of the world's best in meeting the needs of a competitive economy. It also ranks the Irish workforce as one of the most flexible, adaptable, and motivated. Ireland's young workforce has shown a particular flair for collecting, interpreting, and disseminating research information. Major investment in education has provided a skilled, well-educated workforce—Ireland has more than twice the U.S. and European per capita average in science and engineering graduates.

A track record of success

Ireland's success in innovation spans a wide range of businesses and sectors. For example, some of the most exciting Irish-based product development has been in medical technologies. Over half of all medical technologies companies based in Ireland have dedicated R&D centers. Boston Scientific researched and developed the world's first drug-coated stent using researchers in Ireland. Bristol-Myers Squibb's Swords Laboratories is the launch site for several new health care treatments used to treat hypertension, cancer, and HIV/AIDS. GlaxoSmithKline's latest Irish R&D project involves groundbreaking research into gastrointestinal diseases, in collaboration with the Alimentary Pharmabiotic Centre at University College Cork. Recently, Microsoft marked its 20th anniversary in Ireland by opening a new R&D center, creating 100 new jobs. The center is working on a wide range of projects, including Digital Video Broadcasting (DVB) and SmartCard security technology. Intel, a significant supporter of education and training in Ireland, is engaged in several research collaborations with leading Irish universities, including Trinity College Dublin, University College Cork, and Dublin City University. Intel's Irish operation is the global headquarters for the company's Innovation Centres. Analog Devices' long-established R&D operation is heavily integrated into its Irish operation. Its 335-member team has sole responsibility for the global design, manufacture, and supply of value-added high-voltage, mixed-signal CMOS products.

An exciting future of world-class innovation

Alcatel-Lucent Bell Labs, one of the world's most eminent research institutions, has established its Centre for Telecommunications Value-Chain-Driven Research

(continued)

Annex *(Continued)*

in partnership with Trinity College Dublin. It will undertake research aimed at realizing the next generation of telecommunications networks. The Georgia Tech Research Institute's new Irish operation will be a critical component of Ireland's innovation infrastructure. It plans to build up a portfolio of research programs and collaborations with industry, which at full operation will employ 50 highly qualified researchers. Wyeth is establishing a biotherapeutic drug discovery and development research facility at University College Dublin. It will utilize new technologies to discover the next generation of therapeutic biopharmaceuticals for the treatment of a wide variety of diseases. At an academic level, just one illustration of the integration in R&D activity is Dublin City University's Biomedical Diagnostics Institute. It is carrying out cutting-edge research programs focused on the development of next-generation biomedical diagnostic devices. Ireland's success is based on a culture of cooperation and collaboration to win complex, high-value, sophisticated investments. The country's strong business philosophy of inclusiveness, informality, and teamwork are the foundations on which Ireland is fast becoming an important player in the development of global innovation networks.

Sources: Business Week 2004; IDA Ireland.

References

African Development Fund. 2005. *Skills Training and Vocational Education Project—Appraisal Report*, Tunis, Tunisia: African Development Fund.

All India Management Association–High Level Strategic Group. 2003. "India's New Opportunity, 2020." http://www.aima-ind.org/NewPdfs/HLSG_India2020_Executive_Summary.pdf.

Aubert, Jean-Eric. 2006. "The Knowledge Economy: Strategic Issues." World Bank Institute Presentation.

Billetoft, J., M. Powell, and V. Treichel. 2008. *Nigeria: Labour Market Trends and Skills Development*. Washington, DC: World Bank.

Business Monitor International Ltd. 2008. *Nigeria Telecommunications Report Q4.*

Central Bank of Nigeria. 2006. *Annual Report 2006.* Abuja.

Central Bank of Nigeria. 2009. *Communiqué No. 65 of the Monetary Policy Committee Meeting—September 1, 2009.* Abuja.

Cheah, H.M., and T.S. Kahu. 2002. "Building Towards an E-learning Environment in the National Institute of Education." Global Summit.

Clark, N. and R. Sedgwick, "Education in Nigeria." *World Education News & Reviews*, September/October 2004, http://www.wes.org/ewenr/04Sept/Practical.htm.

Dahlman, C. 2008. "Challenges of the Global and Knowledge Economy for Africa." PowerPoint presentation at the Africa Finance and Private Sector Development Department meeting, October 2, 2008. World Bank, Washington DC.

Dahlman, C., and J. Aubert. 2001. *China and the Knowledge Economy.* Washington, DC: World Bank.

D'Costa, A.P. 2003. "Uneven and Combined Development: Understanding Indian Software Exports." *World Development* 31 (1): 211–26.

Economist Intelligence Unit. 2008. *Global Outlook,* London: Economist Intelligence Unit.

Green, M. 2009. "Downturn Hastens Nigeria's Brain Gain." *Financial Times,* August 20.

Fox, L., & A.M. Oviedo. 2008. "Are Skills Rewarded in Sub-Saharan Africa? Determinants of Wages and Productivity in the Manufacturing Sector." Policy Research Working Paper 4688. Washington, DC: World Bank.

Goldman Sachs. 2007. "The N-11—More than an Acronym." Global Economics Paper No. 153.

Haywood, L., and F. Teal. 2008. *Employment, Unemployment, Joblessness and Incomes in Nigeria: 1999-2006.* Oxford, England: Center for the Study of African Economies.

Hepeng, Jia, and Fu Jing. "China praised for its potential as science super power." Accessed January 18, 2007, at www.scidev.net.

Hinchliffe, K. 2002. "Public Expenditures in Education in Nigeria: Issues, Estimates, and Some Implications." Africa Region Human Development Working Papers Series. Washington, DC: World Bank.

Hwa, Ko Kheng. 2003. "Knowledge Powers Singapore Economy." *Information Age.* 30–33.

Iarossi, G., P. Mousley, and I. Radwan. 2008. *An Assessment of the Investment Climate in Nigeria.* Washington, DC: World Bank.

Ibrahim, A. 2006. "Progress on the MDGs in Nigeria. Education—Where Are We?" Presentation at the 12th Annual Nigerian Economic Summit, Abuja, June 7-9.

Isern, J., A. Agbakoba, M. Flaming, J. Mantilla, G. Pellegrini,, and M. Tarazi. 2009. *Access to Finance in Nigeria: Microfinance, Branchless Banking and SME Finance.* Washington, DC: World Bank.

JP Morgan. 2008. "Nigerian Banks." Africa Equity Research Working Paper. http://www.scribd.com/doc/12796880/Nigerian-Banks-Rough-Ride-Ahead-JP-Morgan-2008-Africa-Equity-Research-by-Andrew-Cuffe.

Kingdon, G. 2007. "The Progress of School Education in India." *Oxford Review of Economic Policy* 23 (2): 168–95.

Lovegrove, A., and A. David. Forthcoming. "The Commercial Banking Sector in Nigeria." In *Making Finance Work for Nigeria,* ed. M. Fuchs and I. Radwan. Washington, DC: World Bank.

Mailafia, O. 2008. "Science, Technology and the Knowledge-Driven Society: Policy Options for Nigeria." Presentation at the 18th Public Lecture at Abubakar Tafawa Balewa University, Bauchi State, Nigeria, January 30.

MDG Monitor, http://www.mdgmonitor.org.

National Knowledge Commission, http://www.knowledgecommission.gov.in/default.asp.

National Media. 2007. "Bank to Fund ICT Bureaux," http://www.marsgroupkenya.org/multimedia/?StoryID=163276.

Nigeria, Budget Office of the Federation. 2009a. *2008 Budget.* Abuja.

Nigeria, Budget Office of the Federation. 2009b. *2009 Budget Speech.* Abuja.

Nigeria, Budget Office of the Federation. 2009c. *2009 First Quarter—Budget Implementation Report.* Abuja.

Nworah, U. 2005. *Study on Nigerian Diaspora.* http://www.globalpolitician.com/2682-nigeria.

OECD Observer. Herd, Richard and Sean Dougherty. "China's Economy: A remarkable transformation." 2005

OECD Observer: "Made in China", November 2006 http://www.oecdobserver.org.

Odia, L.O., and S.I. Omofonmwan. 2007. "Educational System in Nigeria: Problems and Prospects." *Journal of Social Sciences* 14 (1): 81–6.

Okoje, J. 2008. *Licensing, Accreditation and Quality Assurance in Nigerian Universities: Achievements and Challenges.* Abuja, Nigeria: National Universities Commission.

Okonjo-Iweala, N., and P. Osafo-Kwaako. 2007. *Nigeria's Economic Reforms: Progress and Challenges.* Washington, DC: Brookings Institution.

Porter, M. 1990. *The Competitive Advantage of Nations.* New York: The Free Press.

Porter, M., G.T. Crocombe, and M.J. Enright. 1991. *Upgrading New Zealand's Competitive Advantage.* Auckland, New Zealand: Oxford University Press.

Pyramid Research. 2007. *From Triple-Play to Quad-Play: Strategies, Business Models and Best Practices.* Rockville, MD: Pyramid Research.

Reynolds, P.D., W.D. Bygrave, E. Autio & others. 2004. "GEM Global Report 2003". www.gemconsortium.org.

Salmi, J. 2009. *The Challenge of Establishing World-Class Universities.* Washington, DC: World Bank.

Söderbom, M., F. Teal, A. Wambugu, and G. Kahyarara. 2006. "The Dynamics of Returns to Education in Kenyan and Tanzanian Manufacturing." *Oxford Bulletin of Economics and Statistics.* Centre for the study of African Economies, Working Paper. 2003 (CSAE-WPS 2003(17)).

Soludo, C. 2008. *Banks and the National Economy: Progress, Challenges and the Road Ahead.* Abuja, Nigeria: Central Bank of Nigeria.

Tan, Kim-Song. 2004. From "Efficiency-Driven to Innovation-Driven Economic Growth: Perspectives from Singapore." Working Paper 15–2004. Singapore Management University School of Economics.

UNICEF, Millennium Development Goals, http://www.unicef.org/mdg/.

Utz, A. 2006. "Fostering Innovation, Productivity and Technological Change: Tanzania in the Knowledge Economy." World Bank Working Papers. Washington, DC: World Bank Institute.

Utz, A., and C. Dahlman. 2005. *India and the Knowledge Economy: Leveraging Strengths and Opportunities.* Washington, DC: World Bank.

Vanguard News Online. http://vanguard.ugr.com.

Vodafone Group. 2009. "India: The Impact of Mobile Phones." Policy Paper Series, Number 9. Vodafone Group. http://www.vodafone.com/etc/medialib/public_policy_series.Par.56572.File.dat/public_policy_series_9.pdf.

Waverman, L., M. Meschi, and M. Fuss. 2005. "The Impact of Telecoms on Economic Growth in Developing Countries." LEGC, London. http://web.si.umich.edu/tprc/papers/2005/450/L%20Waverman-%20Telecoms%20Growth%20in%20Dev.%20Countries.pdf.

Wijesinha, A. 2008. "Testing the Education-Growth Nexus and Investigating Educational Disparities Across Regions: The Case of India." PhD diss., Leeds University Business School.

World Bank 2005a. *India and the Knowledge Economy: Leveraging Strengths and Opportunities.* Washington, DC.

———. 2005b. Zeng, Douglas. China's Employment Challenges and Strategies after the WTO Accession and World Trade Organization. World Bank Policy Research Working Paper 3522. Washington, DC: World Bank.

World Bank. 2006. "Nigeria Science and Technology Education at Post-Basic Level (STEPB): A review of S&T Education in Federally Funded Institutions." Report No. 37973, Washington, DC: World Bank.

World Bank. 2008. *Nigeria 2008—Enterprise Surveys.* Washington, DC: World Bank.

World Bank and International Finance Corporation. 2009. *Doing Business 2010: Reforming through Difficult Times."* Washington, DC: World Bank and International Finance Corporation.

World Bank Education Statistics, http://web.worldbank.org/WBSITE/EXTERNAL/TOPICS/EXTEDUCATION/EXTDATASTATISTICS.html.

World Bank, Knowledge for Development, http://info.worldbank.org/etools/kam2/.

World Economic Forum. 2009. *Global Competitiveness Report.* Geneva, Switzerland: World Economic Forum.

Index

Figures, notes, and tables are indicated by *f*, *n*, and *t*, respectively.

I

ICT (information and communications technology). *See* information infrastructure
Independent Corrupt Practices and Other Related Offences Commission (ICPC), 74
India
  business environment, 108–09
  centers of excellence creation, 28
  cost of doing business, 47
  credit market, 61
  customs delays, 65
  education system, 30, 35, 110–11
  GDP growth, 103
  imbalances in access to education, 43
  information infrastructure, 108, 111–12
  innovation system, 91, 94, 109–10
  knowledge economy strategy, 105–08
  lessons for Nigeria, 113–14
  position in the knowledge economy, 105*f*
  progress towards becoming a knowledge economy, 103–05
  recommendations, 104, 112–13
Indian Institutes of Management (IIMs), 7, 28, 91, 110
Indian Institutes of Technology (ITTS), 7, 28, 91, 110
Indonesia, 47, 65, 73
Industrial Training Fund, 39
information infrastructure
  in China, 129–30
  competitive ICT sector need, 79–80
  in India, 108, 111–12
  international communications, 84–85
  Internet penetration, 83–84
  in Korea, 140–41
  lag in ICT infrastructure for education, 34–35
  as a pillar of the knowledge economy, 19, 20
  policy and regulatory environment, 85–86
  recommendations, 86–87
  in Singapore, 155–56
  in South Africa, 81
  technologies' impact on the economy, 5–6, 79, 85
  telecom sector growth, 80–82

innovation system
  brain drain reduction, 97–99
  in China, 94, 117–24, 126
  components of, 89
  countries comparison, 90–92
  in Egypt, 91
  firm-level capacity to absorb technology, 93–94
  impact on an economy, 6
  improving the innovation culture, 95–97
  in India, 91, 94, 109–10
  industrial clusters, 98–99
  in-firm training, 97
  innovation process steps, 90
  in Ireland, 158–61
  in Korea, 138–40
  patents and, 93
  as a pillar of the knowledge economy, 19, 20
  private sector spending on R&D, 94–95
  recommendations, 99–100
  regional integration through ECOWAS, 97
  in Singapore, 147–53
  in South Africa, 90, 91
Intellectual Property Office of Singapore (IPOS), 150
intellectual property rights, 4, 93, 150–51, 152
International Adult Literacy Survey, 40
Internet penetration, 83–84
Investment Climate Assessment, World Bank, 94
Ireland, 158–61

K

KAM. *See* Knowledge Assessment Methodology
KEI (Knowledge Economy Index), 20
Kenya
  corruption in, 73
  cost of doing business, 47
  credit market, 61
  customs delays, 65
  education system, 30
  knowledge economy comparison, 23
Knowledge Assessment Methodology (KAM)
  business environment pillar, 4
  defined, 19
  education system pillar, 2–3